Elementary Biblical Hebrew

An Introduction to the Language and its History

BY CHET RODEN
LIBERTY UNIVERSITY

Bassim Hamadeh, CEO and Publisher
Michael Simpson, Vice President of Acquisitions
Jamie Giganti, Senior Managing Editor
Miguel Macias, Senior Graphic Designer
David Miano, Specialist Acquisitions Editor
Monika Dziamka, Project Editor
Brian Fahey, Licensing Specialist
Rachel Singer, Associate Editor

Copyright © 2017 by Cognella, Inc. All rights reserved. No part of this publication may be reprinted, reproduced, transmitted, or utilized in any form or by any electronic, mechanical, or other means, now known or hereafter invented, including photocopying, microfilming, and recording, or in any information retrieval system without the written permission of Cognella, Inc.

Trademark Notice: Product or corporate names may be trademarks or registered trademarks, and are used only for identification and explanation without intent to infringe.

Cover image copyright © 2009 by iStockphoto LP / Peter Zelei.

Printed in the United States of America

ISBN: 978-1-63189-211-0 (pbk) / 978-1-63189-212-7 (br)

TABLE of CONTENTS

Chapter 1   2
Rationale, History of the Alphabet, Alphabet: Part 1

Chapter 2   14
Iron Age Inscriptions, Alphabet: Part 2

Chapter 3   34
Vowels

Chapter 4   46
Nouns, Syllabification, Accents, and Reading

Chapter 5   56
Definite Article, Inseparable Preposition, Vav Conjunction, and Word Studies (Nouns)

Chapter 6   68
Pronouns, Construct States, and Adjectives

Chapter 7   78
Verbs: Part 1

Chapter 8   88
Verbs: Part 2

Rationale, History of the Alphabet, Alphabet: Part 1

1.1 Rationale for Learning Biblical Hebrew

One of the questions most often asked of Hebrew professors has to be, "Why do we need to learn Hebrew?" Students are usually wondering if the reward is worth the effort. Let me say that learning Biblical Hebrew is indeed worth the effort. Consider these brief reasons for learning Biblical Hebrew.

1. **Hebrew is the language through which God chose to reveal himself and to create his people.** Exodus 31:18 says, *"When He had finished speaking with him upon Mount Sinai, He gave Moses the two tablets of the testimony, tablets of stone, written by the finger of God."* Surely if God thought it important enough to use Hebrew as the writing medium for his self-revelation to humanity, it should be important enough for us to learn.

2. **Hebrew is the language of the Scriptures used by Jesus and the apostles.** While Greek and Aramaic became commonly spoken languages of Jesus and the apostles, the language of the temple and synagogue was Hebrew. Recall the episode in Nazareth when Jesus was in the synagogue. Luke tells us that Jesus

   entered the synagogue on the Sabbath, and stood up to read. And the book of the prophet Isaiah was handed to Him. And He opened the book and found the place where it was written, "The Spirit of the Lord is upon Me. Because He anointed Me to preach the gospel to the poor. He has sent Me to proclaim release to the captives, and recovery of sight to the blind, to set free those who are oppressed, to proclaim the favorable year of the Lord." And He closed the book, gave it back to the attendant and sat down. (Luke 4:16–20a)

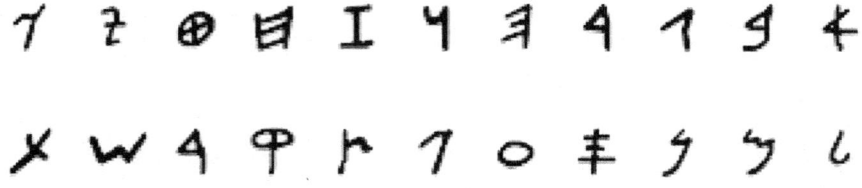

FIGURE 1.1.1. ANCIENT HEBREW ALPHABET
Copyright in the Public Domain.

Thus, we cannot simply overlook the language of the text that Jesus and the apostles called Scripture.

3. **Knowing Biblical Hebrew leads to a deeper, more personal understanding of the Old Testament.** The multitude of English translations tells of the significance of understanding the ancient languages of the Bible. Biblical translators continually try to improve our understanding of the biblical texts through new translations. But, when studying deeply and personally, having a foundational knowledge of the language is very rewarding for a reader. That enhanced study becomes even more personal than when depending on another's translation. Only those who take the time to learn the language will discover this amazing benefit.

4. **Knowing Biblical Hebrew provides the tool for biblical study at the word and sentence level.** Understanding the nuances of words will reveal the depth of the Hebrew language. Studying how words, sentences, and paragraphs work together (technically called syntax), will prevent making embarrassing mistakes of interpretation and understanding.

1.2 A Brief History of the Alphabet

Before you begin learning the Hebrew alphabet, we should first consider the history of writing and the alphabet. Biblical Hebrew is a product of several factors in the history of writing and communicating through writing, which is widely recognized to have begun in

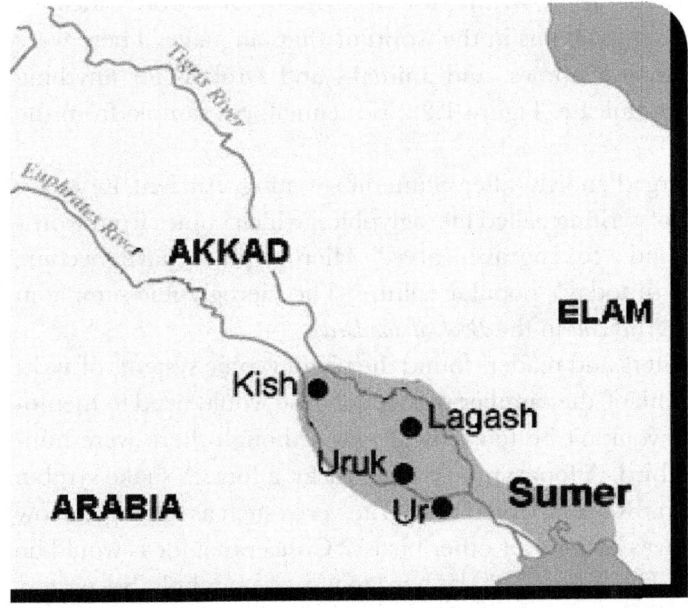

FIGURE 1.2.1. MAP OF SOUTHEASTERN MESOPOTAMIA
Fionn / Wikimedia Commons / Copyright in the Public Domain.

FIGURE 1.2.2. TWENTY-SIXTH CENTURY BC CUNEIFORM SAMPLE
Copyright in the Public Domain.

Sumer. The first written communication that we know of is from Sumer and dates to the fourth millennium BC. Sumer is located in southeastern Mesopotamia near the Persian Gulf.

The Akkadian language developed after Sumerian. Both Sumerian and Akkadian used a cuneiform writing system (wedge-shaped characters) which, in the beginning, was pictographic in nature. Pictographic writing uses a "symbol for a word" idea, or logograms. Each symbol represented items in the world of that language. There were different symbols for men, women, homes, and animals; and symbols for anything the writer would need to communicate. Figure 1.2.2 is a cuneiform sample from the twenty-sixth century BC.

Egyptian writing also emerged shortly after Sumerian writing. Ancient Egyptian also used a pictographic form of writing called hieroglyphics, which comes from words meaning "religious/sacred" and "to engrave/carve." Hieroglyphics have become synonymous with Egypt, even in today's popular culture. The hieroglyphic sample in Figure 1.2.3 came from the *Papyrus Ani* in the *Book of the Dead*.

As time moved forward, writers and readers found the pictographic systems of writing very difficult to master. Think of the number of symbols one would need to memorize in such a system. Nouns wouldn't be too difficult, even though there were hundreds. A bird symbol means a bird. A foot symbol would mean a foot. A snake symbol would mean a snake, and so on. But how would one write verbs such as "flying"? How would a writer say, "The bird was flying over other birds"? Conceptual ideas would be even more difficult than verbs. Thoughts would be hard to write as symbols. So, writers invented different groupings of symbols to indicate verbs, concepts, and abstract things. But this led to an even greater difficulty for reading and writing. Memorizing all the

FIGURE 1.2.3. Hieroglyphic sample from the *Papyrus Ani*
Copyright in the Public Domain.

pictographic symbols was a daunting task, and still is for scholars today. In fact, the systems became very unwieldy and limiting. Only certain people could receive the education for understanding these systems. So perhaps it was inevitable that the cuneiform and hieroglyphic forms of writing would ultimately be changed and simplified.

Near the end of the second millennium BC, writing systems had evolved to use what is now called the acrophonic principle. Whereas the cuneiform and hieroglyphic systems used the "symbol for word" system, alphabets using the acrophonic principle, which changed to a "symbol for sound" system, began emerging during this time. For example, the word for house was "bet." The cuneiform and hieroglyphic system wrote the symbol for a house and the reader would read "bet" with the understanding that the word "house" was being communicated. The acrophonic system used the same symbol for house, but instead the reader understood it as the sound "b," which is the first letter of "bet."

Pictographic = symbol equals word = *BET*
Acrophonic = symbol equals first letter sound of the corresponding word = *B*

The acrophonic principle was the driving force behind the development of the Sinaitic and Northwest Semitic alphabets. Both arose near the beginning of the second millennium BC.

The Northwest Semitic alphabet is generally called the Phoenician alphabet. The Phoenician alphabet made use of the cuneiform writing style and the acrophonic principle. Scribes used cuneiform wedge-shaped writing to make the acrophonic symbols. Thus the Phoenician alphabet used a blended acrophonic cuneiform system.

Recently, Orly Goldwasser presented an intriguing theory on the rise of the Sinaitic alphabet from hieroglyphs in her article, "How the Alphabet Was Born from Hieroglyphs." The description below is a synopsis of her theory.

During the reigns of Amenemhet III and IV (1853–1808 and 1808–1799 BC), Egypt was at the height of her power. There was an active trade during this time among Egypt, Canaan, and Mesopotamia. Part of this trade was in part due to the turquoise mining in Serabit el-Khadem, which is located in the desolate regions of the Sinai Peninsula.

At the top of the mountains at Serabit el-Khadem, archaeologists in the early 1900s discovered the remains of an ancient Egyptian temple dedicated to the goddess Hathor. Hathor is the Egyptian Mistress of Turquoise. The temple was founded just prior to the reigns of Amenemhet III and IV, between 1953 and 1908 BC. The temple continued in existence until around 1100 BC. When the turquoise mine was a great source of trade and economic stability, the temple of Hathor rose to a striking position of importance, because the workers sought the blessings of Hathor. Thus, the temple was enlarged during this time period.

On the pathway leading to the Hathor temple, the workers of the mine built shrines and carved hieroglyphic inscriptions to Hathor. These engravings were requests for blessings and protection in their endeavors.

An interesting twist to how this contributed to the rise of the Proto-Sinaitic alphabet is that the people who left the inscriptions were both Egyptian and Canaanite. During

FIGURE 1.2.4. Part of the pathway leading up to the Temple of Hathor. Photo by Roland Unger.
Copyright © 2009 by Roland Unger, (CC BY-SA 3.0) at: http://commons.wikimedia.org/wiki/File%3ASerabitSouthernPart.jpg.

this time period, the economic situation caused Egypt to be more tolerant towards the Canaanites, due to their shared interest in the turquoise trade. According to Goldwasser, the expedition lists contain the names of many who were called "interpreters," which would give strong evidence that there was a language barrier between the Egyptians and the Canaanites. Her theory is that it was this interaction between the Egyptians and Canaanites that gave rise to the invention of an alphabetic writing system.

As noted earlier, writing systems like Egyptian hieroglyphs and Mesopotamian cuneiform required the memorization of hundreds of signs in order to write or read. But an alphabetic writing system uses fewer than thirty signs. Thus, Goldwasser poses the theory that while the Canaanites are to be given credit for inventing the alphabet, it was the Egyptian hieroglyphs that provided the trigger and means that made the invention of the alphabet possible.

Excavators Sir William Flinders Petrie and his wife Hilda Petrie are recognized for noticing the transition from hieroglyphs to alphabet at Serabit el-Khadem. Hilda Petrie noticed that among the writings there were symbols that were not really hieroglyphs. But it was Sir Alan Gardiner who began to piece the transition puzzle together some ten years later.

Gardiner pointed out a group of four signs that were often repeated in these unusual scripts along the pathway to Hathor's temple. He argued that the signs were a series of four letters in an alphabetic script that represented a word in Canaanite. That word was "Baalat," which means "the mistress." Gardiner deduced that this word referred to the goddess Hathor.

The artifact that prompted Gardiner's theory was a small sphinx with a bilingual inscription engraved in Egyptian and in a "new" script (Figure 1.2.5).

The four-letter group consisted of symbols for a house, an eye, an ox goad, and a cross. You will notice these letters in Figure 1.2.5. The grouping that caught Gardiner's attention is located on the base of the sphinx, just under the torso (the white-colored text). The same letters are also on the opposite side of the sphinx, but cannot be seen in this image. The house looks like a square box. The eye looks similar to an English "A." The ox goad is similar to the Arabic number "9," and the cross is the last symbol on the right and looks like a cross or "t." The letters should be read from left to right. Gardiner realized that each picture did not stand for the depicted word, but instead depicted the initial sound of the word or the first letter of that particular word. In other words, the writer was using the acrophonic principal, and not the pictographic principle. The drawings did not represent the word, only the initial sounds.

Goldwasser argues that since the alphabetic script retained its pictorial forms for hundreds of years, it made reading and writing more available to the uneducated. Those who were not socially educated could remember the thirty or so alphabetic pictographs. To remember the alphabet, all one had to do was memorize the pictures. The picture would lead them to a word, which then helped to recreate the form and sound

FIGURE 1.2.5. SERABIT SPHINX
Copyright © by The British Museum Images.

of the letter. Alphabetic reading and writing followed from that. So, in the melting pot of the Serabit El-Khadem mines, where literate and illiterate, Egyptian and Canaanite, came together in the worship and veneration of Hathor, the transition from Egyptian hieroglyphs to an alphabetic script began.

At this point, however, the primary thing for you to take away from the above discussion is that, during the second millennium BC, there was a transition in writing from pictographic systems to an acrophonic system. That evolution ultimately led to alphabetic writing. The evolution occurred in the Sinai regions of the Southern Levant and north in Mesopotamian regions over hundreds of years. The alphabet did not become settled and stationary until the late parts of the second millennium BC. During that millennium, the Phoenician alphabet became the most dominant and popular alphabetic script and became the one of the primary bases for the Hebrew alphabet. Figure 1.2.6 is a comparison chart of the Proto-Sinaitic, Phoenician, and Hebrew alphabets.

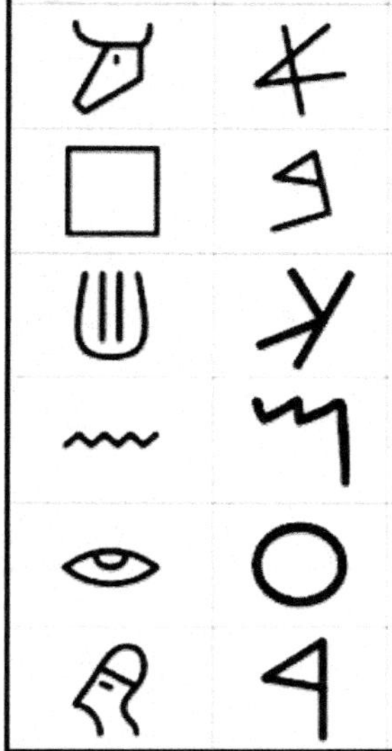

Proto-Sinaitic	Phoenician	Hebrew	Phoen. name
🐂	✶	א	ʾalp "ox"
☐	⌐	ב	bet "house"
🖐	⨯	כ	kap "hand"
〰	ⵏ	מ	mem "water"
👁	O	ע	ʿen "eye"
𓁶	⟜	ר	roʾš "head"

Figure 1.2.6. Comparison of some alphabetic symbols with Hebrew

1.3 The Hebrew Alphabet (Part 1)

When learning to read any language, the alphabet of that language must be memorized. Biblical Hebrew is no different. Below is about half of the consonantal alphabet of Biblical Hebrew. The remainder of the alphabet will be learned in Chapter 2. Also, the vowels are a system unto themselves and will be addressed in a later chapter. When learning the alphabet, you should memorize the symbol, its name, and its sound. For example, the name of the symbol ב is Bet. It is pronounced like the English letter "b." The symbol Aleph (א) however, is silent. Take plenty of time to memorize the consonants below.

Hints:
- With just a couple of exceptions (silent letters), the names of the letters will tell you the sound. Bet = b, Gimel = g, Dalet = d, and so on.
- Learn the alphabet in order, just like you learned the English alphabet.
- There are Aleph-Bet songs on YouTube that might help you by putting music to the alphabet. This is much like how English readers learn the English alphabet song. Simply search for the Aleph-Bet song on the Internet and choose your favorite.

Symbol	Name	Sound
א	Aleph	Silent
ב	Bet	b as in boy
ג	Gimel	g as in give
ד	Dalet	d as in dog
ה	Hey	h as in hay/hey
ו	Vav	v as in vine (some pronounce this as waw; w as in water)
ז	Zayin	z as in zoo
ח	Chet	"ch" as in Bach
ט	Tet	t as in tent
י	Yod	y as in yoyo (soe say the ythis as yud, but still has the y sound)
כ	Kaph	k as in king; ך = the final form Kaph. It will always be at the end of a word.

1.4 Writing Block Letters

Your handwriting of Biblical Hebrew will not look like the printed fonts you will be seeing in print. Yours will most likely be blockier. But, strive to be clear and precise. Be careful to make each letter distinct. Take care not to make letters look alike.

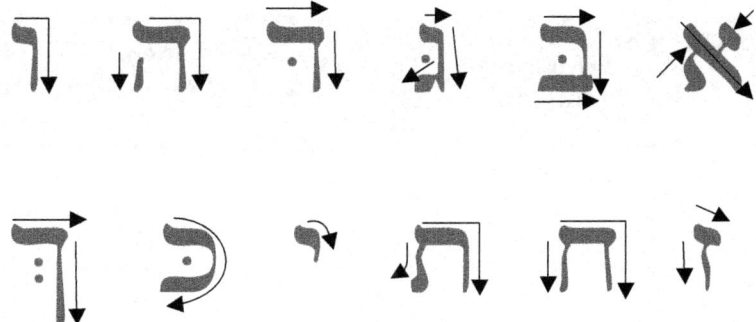

1.5 Exercises

1. Practice writing the letters. Remember, Hebrew is written and read from right to left. So practice writing the letters beginning on the right side of the provided space. Write each letter enough times to become proficient. If the space provided is not enough, use your own lined paper to practice.

Writing Space Be careful and precise	Letter Name	Hebrew Consonant
		א
		ב
		ג
		ד
		ה
		ו
		ז
		ח
		ט
		י
		כ

2. What is the pictographic principle of writing?

3. What is the acrophonic principle of writing?

_____

4. Where was the first place writing appeared in the Ancient Near East?

_____

5. What are the two writing systems in the Ancient Near East that transitioned from the pictographic to acrophonic system of writing?

_____

6. What was the location in the Sinai where the transition from hieroglyphs to an acrophonic system occurred?

_____

7. Who was the person who first noticed the repetition of the four-character word that led to the discovery of the transition from hieroglyphs to the acrophonic system?

_____

1.6 Further Reading

Albright, William F. 1966. *The Proto-Sinaitic Inscriptions and Their Decipherment*. Harvard Theology Studies 22. Cambridge, MA: Harvard University Press.

Goldwasser, Orly. 2010. "How the Alphabet Was Born from Hieroglyphs." *Biblical Archaeology Review* March/April: 36–50.

Rollston, Christopher. 2010. *Writing and Literacy in the World of Ancient Israel: Epigraphic Evidence from the Iron Age*. Atlanta, GA: Society of Biblical Literature.

Iron Age Inscriptions, Alphabet: Part 2

2.1 A Brief History of Hebrew

All the details of the history of Biblical Hebrew are not crystal clear. The process is much better understood than the details of that process. The lack of Old Testament manuscripts due to deterioration is one of the factors clouding the issue. Making matters more difficult was the Jewish process of destroying older copies of biblical manuscripts so as not to profane them and the name of the Lord. Thus, there are no extant manuscripts of the complete Hebrew Bible until the tenth century AD. Even among the Dead Sea Scrolls, there is not a manuscript of the entire Hebrew Bible. There are many great fragments and one incredible, complete scroll of Isaiah. But there are none of the complete Hebrew Bible. So, the time gap between our first complete Hebrew Bible and the generally accepted completion of the Hebrew Bible is twelve hundred to thirteen hundred years.

In its original form, the Hebrew Bible was a consonantal text. It did not have written vowels. The vowel sounds and word pronunciations were passed along verbally. So you can imagine there would be some pronunciation and word meaning issues. Look at these examples, using English, as illustration of how potential mistakes could occur:

Example:

Consonantal	With Vowels
Th tr ws rnd	The tree was round

But that is not the only way the sentence could be read and understood. The sentence could also be read and understood as:

Th tr ws rnd	The tree was ruined
Th tr ws rnd	The tire was ruined
Th tr ws rnd	The tire was round

So, it is easy to see that consonantal texts can be difficult to understand with exactness. Thus, as time progressed, groups of Jewish scholars dating as far back as Ezra sought to standardize the understanding and pronunciation of the Hebrew biblical texts by making notes around the consonantal text to explain pronunciations and meanings. Those notations are called Masora. The groups who wrote those notes are called Masoretes. Along with the notations about the text, the Masoretes also developed a vowel system called "vowel pointing." This vowel pointing system, which will be discussed in detail later, functioned around the established consonantal text without adding to, taking away from, or altering the consonantal texts. By the tenth century AD there was an accepted text of the Hebrew Bible, which is today known as the Masoretic text. The Masoretic text has become the standard Hebrew text used today, although there are other academic texts in use as well.

While we did not have a manuscript of the complete Hebrew Bible until very recently, the people of Israel had been reading and writing in Hebrew for more than two thousand years prior. Let's take a look at some of the more famous inscriptions that have been discovered that date within the Israelite period (Iron Age).

2.2 Iron Age Inscriptions

As discussed in Chapter 1, an alphabetic writing system had developed by the end of the second millennium BC. That time frame corresponds generally to what archaeologists have termed the Iron Age. The Iron Age spanned the years 1200 to 586 BC, with some minor variations. It should be noted that the Iron Age is divided into time sections that are being debated currently. But for our discussions here, there is no need to argue the divisions. Just let it suffice to say that as the Iron Age began, alphabetic writing had firmly established itself as the writing style of choice in the Ancient Near East and the Levant. As Israel was establishing itself as a nation, the Hebrew language and writing grew out of the Proto-Sinaitic and Phoenician alphabets. While some argue for an earlier date, there is little debate that by the ninth century BC, Hebrew had become the national language of the nation of Israel.

In the following pages, we will discuss some Iron Age inscriptions found in and near Israel. There have been a good number of Iron Age inscriptions unearthed that help us understand the language of the Hebrews and its development. Although there are several Iron Age inscriptions available to us now, it is small in comparison to the number of Iron Age excavation sites in Israel. The fragility of the writing materials is the biggest enemy of finding ancient writing in Israel. Papyrus is only rarely preserved in Israel, due to the nation's humidity and dampness. Of course, ostraca (pottery fragments that contain writing either scratched or in ink) and engraved inscriptions occur in a larger quantity, due to their durability. But, since ostraca were often written in organic ink, the ink has often disappeared or is even washed off after being excavated. Ink-written ostraca survive only in rare situations.

Nonetheless, there is an interesting group of Iron Age inscriptions, which are fascinating to study and of which you should be aware. Some of the more recent findings have captured the attention of a worldwide audience and have great significance concerning the Bible and the nation of Israel. Below are a few representative examples.

Ophel Inscription[1]

Eilat Mazar is the chief archaeologist excavating in the Ophel, or the City of David, just south of the Temple Mount in Jerusalem. During excavations in 2012, the team unearthed a large building that contained seven broken pithoi (storage pots).[2] Around the neck of one of those was an inscription incised by the potter prior to the firing of the pottery. Dr. Shmuel Ahituv was responsible for the initial deciphering of the letters. "The inscription is incised in a Proto-Canaanite/Early Canaanite script of the eleventh-tenth centuries BCE."[3] The inscription is somewhat enigmatic, but has been thought to mean "pot," followed by a personal name.[4] Mazar states that the inscription is most likely the oldest inscription ever found in Jerusalem.[5] Christopher Rollston sum-

---

1   Eilat Mazar, "Earliest Alphabetical Inscription Found in Jerusalem," http://www.keytodavidscity.com/earliest-alphabetical-inscription-found-in-jerusalem-3/. This site offers a short video explaining the finding and examination of the inscription.
2   Eilat Mazar, Shmuel Ahituv, and David Ben-Schlomo, "An Inscribed Pithos from the Ophel," *Israel Exploration Journal* 63, no. 1 (2013): 39–49.
3   Ibid., 39.
4   Christopher Rollston, "The Decipherment of the New 'Incised Jerusalem Pithos,'" http://www.rollstonepigraphy.com/?p=561 (July 11, 2013).
5   Mazar, "Earliest Alphabetical Inscription," http://www.keytodavidscity.com/earliest-alphabetical-inscription-found-in-jerusalem-3/.

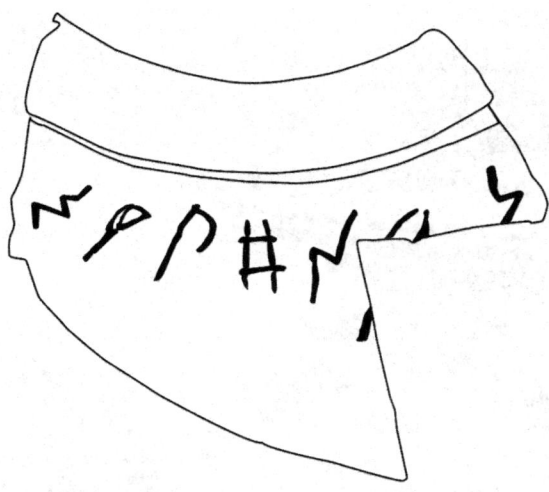

Figure 2.2.1.
Copyright © 2010 by Cristopher Rollston. Reprinted with permission.

marizes the importance of the inscription, saying, "Of course, I personally would be very disinclined to 'build a kingdom upon this potsherd.' But I would wish to state that this is an inscription that fits nicely into, and augments, the totality of our epigraphic evidence for the early Iron Age."[6] Since all indications point to an eleventh/tenth century BC creation of the pot and inscription, this inscription would be in the general vicinity and time period of King David of the Bible.

Goliath Inscription[7]

Biblical Gath has been identified as the modern-day archaeological site of Tell es-Safi. In 1996, Aren Maeir began excavations at Tell es-Safi. Maeir determined that the city of Gath was indeed inhabited by the Philistines during the Iron Age, and particularly during the reign of David. Maeir could make this determination through several evidences, but one of the main things was the pottery. The Philistines had a distinct pottery type that is consistent with Mycenaean pottery types. In the earliest Philistine settlement layers, the pottery proved to be imported—brought with them perhaps in the migration from the northern Mediterranean regions. But neutron analyses of later pottery have shown that the Philistines kept the pottery forms of their Aegean homeland, while using clay from the local area of southwest Palestine.

---

6   Rollston, "The Decipherment," http://www.rollstonepigraphy.com/?p=561 (July 11, 2013).
7   Aren Maeir, "Excavating Philistine Gath: Have We Found Goliath's Hometown?" *Biblical Archaeology Review* 27, no. 6 (Nov/Dec 2001): 22. Maeir, "Comment on the news item in *BAR* on the 'Goliath Inscription,'" https://gath.wordpress.com/2006/02/16/comment-on-the-news-item-in-bar-on-the-goliath-inscription/ (February 16, 2006). For a rebuttal see, Christopher A. Rollston, "An Ancient Medium in the Modern Media: Sagas of Semitic Inscriptions," in *Archaeology, Bible, Politics, and the Media*, ed. Eric and Carol Myers (Winona Lake, IN: Eisenbrauns, 2012), 122–38.

FIGURE 2.2.2.
Copyright © 2010 by Ori~ / Wikimedia Commons. Reprinted with permission.

Perhaps the most fascinating finds from Tell es-Safi occurred in 2005 when Maeir's team unearthed an ostracon. Again, ostraca are pottery sherds that have been written on. Ostraca are somewhat common throughout Israel, but this particular one is of great significance pertaining to the David and Goliath story.

While digging in an archaeological strata that dated to around 950 to 900 BC, Maeir's team discovered an ostraca with a name engraved on it that is an etymological cousin to the name Goliath. The pottery on which the writing was found is a type that dates to the same time as the strata in which it was found. And even further, the writing style itself dates the inscription to the tenth century BC. So, in the tenth century BC, some fifty to one hundred years after the setting of David and Goliath, in the very city described to be the hometown of the biblical Goliath, an inscription that has the etymological cousin to the name Goliath was written on a piece of pottery. Pretty amazing, isn't it?

Still, even if the piece of pottery had an overwhelmingly and conclusively established name of Goliath written on it, that still would not prove the David and Goliath story in the Bible to be true. What does it prove? Well it tells us that the name Goliath, and its derivative cousins (think of Mike, Michael, Michelle, Mick, Mickey), were names used by Philistines during the time the David and Goliath story is told to have happened in the Bible. That is a very important component of the biblical story of Goliath.

Khirbet Qeiyafa Inscription[8]

Qeiyafa is a relatively new site excavated by Yosef Garfinkel and Saar Ganor. It is an imposing Israelite fort on the border of Israel and Philistia. The site dates to the late eleventh to early tenth century BC. It was occupied during this period only, and was then abandoned until the Hellenistic period. Thus the dating is unquestioned.

The most exciting find from Qeiyafa, to date, is an ostracon found near the city gate. It is a 6-by-6-inch inscription on a broken piece of pottery. The ink has faded, which made the translation difficult, but it was translated by Haggai Misgav. A few things seem certain:

1. The script is Proto-Canaanite or Proto-Sinaitic. They are the same crude alphabetic letter forms derived from Egyptian hieroglyphs, like those found in the Serabit turquoise mine area.

2. The ostracon is the oldest Hebrew inscription ever discovered.

3. The ostracon establishes Hebrew literacy in the Israelite population as early as the Davidic and Solomonic kingdoms.

4. Unlike later Hebrew, this script is written left to right. Early scripts were often written in different directions, even vertical.

FIGURE 2.2.3.
Copyright © 2011 by Michael Netzer, (CC BY-SA 3.0) at: http://commons.wikimedia.org/wiki/File:Khirbet_Qeiyafa_Ostracon.jpg.

---

8 Hershel Shanks, "Prize Find: Oldest Hebrew Inscription," *Biblical Archaeology Review* March/April (2010): 51–54. All the information for this section is derived from Shanks' article.

5. Some letter forms are still fluid, such as the aleph, which faces different directions in different parts of the same inscription.

6. Each of the five lines of text has a horizontal line beneath it.

Gezer Calendar

The Gezer calendar is engraved on a small limestone tablet found during the Gezer excavations of 1908. It is possibly an exercise for a pupil, since the text is not written continuously, but in lines. The text lists the twelve months, which are further defined by the agricultural activities carried out in each month. This results in a catalogue of farming activities throughout the course of the year.

> Two months (is) harvesting,
> Two months (is) sowing,
> Two months (is) late sowing,
> One month (is) cutting flax,
> One month (is) cereal harvesting,
> One month (is) cutting and measuring,
> Two months (is) vintage,
> One month (is) harvesting of summer fruit …

FIGURE 2.2.4.
Copyright © 2014 by oncenawhile / Wikimedia Commons, (CC BY-SA 3.0) at: http://commons.wikimedia.org/wiki/File:Gezer_calendar_close_up.jpg

FIGURE 2.2.5.

House of David Inscription

The House of David inscription is one of the most pivotal finds in all of biblical archaeology, and its finding is a remarkable story in its own right. *Biblical Archaeology Review* recounts the story in its March/April 1994 issue.[9] The inscription was uncovered at Tel Dan, which is known in the Bible as the city of Dan. Dan was the most northern city of what we think of as Israel. Dan was once a Canaanite city named Laish and was overthrown, resettled, and renamed by the Israelite tribe of Dan sometime around 1100 BC. As the Canaanite city Laish, it was impressive. Laish had massive earthen ramparts and walls from the Middle Bronze Age to help defend it.

In the dig season of 1993, excavation team surveyor Gila Cook was standing in an Iron Age plaza that had been unearthed in the previous days. Because of the way the sun reflected off one of the basalt stones in the wall, Cook saw letters on it. She called for the dig director, Avraham Biran, who confirmed they had found an inscription. This inscription would create a stir bigger than what they could have imagined.

The stone that had the inscription was part of a victory monument called a stele, which commemorated the defeat of Dan by an Aramean devotee of the god Hadad.

---

9   Hershel Shanks, "'David' Found at Dan," *Biblical Archaeology Review* 20 (March/April 1994): 26–39. See also David Noel Freedman and Jeffrey C. Geoghegan, "'House of David' Is There!" *Biblical Archaeology Review* 21 (March/April 1995): 78–79; Andre Lemaire, "The Tel Dan Stela as a Piece of Royal Historiography," *Journal for the Study of the Old Testament* 81 (December 1998): 3–14; and Avraham Biran, *Biblical Dan* (Jerusalem: Israel Exploration Society, 1994).

The stele had been broken in antiquity and this particular part was used in the building of a wall. There were two pieces found, containing thirteen lines of clearly identifiable text. The writer of the inscription tells of capturing horses and chariots at Dan. Furthermore, he claims to have killed the "king of Israel" and someone who is "of the House of David." The phrases "king of Israel" and "House of David" are very clear and legible. So for the first time in history, there was an extra-biblical reference to the king of Israel and the House of David.

Moabite Stone/Mesha Stele[10]

The discovery of the Moabite Stone dates to 1868, just after the conclusion of the American Civil War. The stone itself is an inscribed black basalt stone, rectangular

FIGURE 2.2.6.

Copyright © 2012 by Mbzt / Wikimedia Commons, (CC BY 3.0) at: http://commons.wikimedia.org/wiki/File%3AP1120870_Louvre_st%C3%A8le_de_M%C3%A9sha_AO5066_rwk.JPG

10 Siegfried H. Horn, "Why the Moabite Stone Was Blown to Pieces," *Biblical Archaeology Review* 12, no. 3 (May/June 1986): 50–61; André Lemaire, "'House of David' Restored in Moabite Inscription," *Biblical Archaeology Review* 20, no. 3 (May/June 1994): 30–37.

in shape, with a rounded top. It is housed in the Louvre in Paris, France. Although there had been some helpful early translations, according to André Lemaire, until 1994 nobody had done a definitive scholarly translation of the inscription on the stone. In 1994, after working for seven years on the project, André Lemaire announced he would be publishing the definitive edition. One of the more fascinating elements of Lemaire's translation was his discovery that the Moabite stone's Early Aramaic inscription contained the phrase, "the House of David," much like the Tel Dan inscription did. So, within a two year span, there were two corroborating, extra-biblical inscriptions published which refer to the House of David.

The Samaria Ostraca

In a side building inside the palace compound of Samaria, a total of seventy-five written fragments were found. Some of them, however, were not legible. These ostraca contain short notes about deliveries of oil and wine, giving the year of the reign of an unknown king, and the names of the sender and recipient. On some, the sender is identified with a place name, but sometimes by the tribal name. The recipients were probably court officials, who would have been receiving the goods personally or as tribute paid to the court. Basically, the texts are administrative in nature.

The Siloam Inscription

The Siloam Inscription relates to the hewing of the tunnel referred to in 2 Kings 20:20 and 2 Chronicles 32:30. Hezekiah feared an Assyrian siege of Jerusalem so, to insure a good water supply, he ordered the digging of a tunnel from the Gihon Spring to a catch basin inside the city wall. The catch pool was later called the pool of Siloam. The inscription recalls the workers tunneling from both ends simultaneously and meeting underground. The inscription celebrates the technical feat achieved by the workers.

It was once believed that the tunnelers followed a small fissure in the bedrock, which allowed the water to seep from the Gihon Spring to the area of the pool. Thus, they were able to meet at the same place without the aid of the modern equipment we have at our disposal.[11] But a more recent theory, proposed by Amos Frumkin and Aryeh Shimron,[12] argues strongly that the route of the tunnel did not always follow a karstic crack. Frumkin and Shimron argue that the tunnelers were using acoustic communication from above. The workers in the tunnel followed the sound that was conducted by

---

11   Dan Gill, "Subterranean Water Works of Biblical Jerusalem: Adaptation of a Karst System," *Science* 254 (1991): 1467; Gill, "Jerusalem's Underground Water Systems: How They Met: Geology Solves Long-Standing Mystery of Hezekiah's Tunnelers," *Biblical Archaeology Review* 20, no. 4 (July/Aug 1994): 20–33.
12   Amos Frumkin and Aryeh Shimron, "Tunnel Engineering in the Iron Age: Geoarchaeology of the Siloam Tunnel, Jerusalem," *Journal of Archaeological Science* 33 (2006): 227–37.

workers pounding on the bedrock from above. This theory explains the areas of the tunnel where there are no indications of a karstic crack, as well as the path deviations due to thicker overburden layers between the tunnelers and surface guidance teams.

The Siloam Inscription is the only building inscription from this period. It was set on a smooth surface inside the tunnel that is now known as Hezekiah's tunnel. The Siloam inscription was discovered in 1880, but removed in 1890. As it was being removed, it was broken into several pieces. The inscription is now housed in the Museum of Antiquities in Istanbul, Turkey.

Inscriptions of Kuntillet 'Ajrud

At an Iron Age fortress at Kuntillet 'Ajrud, located thirty miles southeast of Kadesh-Barnea, there were found some inscriptions on the plaster of walls, on large pithoi, and on stone vessels. These inscriptions are accompanied by numerous drawings of gods, humans, animals, and a variety of religious and sexual figures. These inscriptions give us invaluable insight into the popular religion of ancient Israel.

Elephantine Papyri

A large hoard of Aramaic papyri was discovered on the island of Elephantine in the Nile. It contains letters, marriage contracts, certificates of purchase, and other economic texts from the Jewish colony there. One of the letters was written to the governor of Judah asking permission to rebuild the Jewish Temple on Elephantine.

FIGURE 2.2.7.
Copyright in the Public Domain.

FIGURE 2.2.8.

The Arad Ostraca

Arad is located in the Negev region of Israel, which has a very dry climate. Because of this, several ostraca have been preserved in a fortified location. The individual pieces from the various strata of the fortress comprise letters as well as lists of names of persons and places, after which numerals are often written. Of note is a group of letters addressed to Elyashib, who is known from seal inscriptions and was probably the last commander of the Arad fortress, meaning that he was directly responsible to the king or another high official in Jerusalem. One of the letters orders troops to be sent from Arad to attest to the infiltration of Edomites and to defend a couple of cities that were being threatened. These events date to the sixth century BC. Other ostraca are administrative in nature, giving insight into the administration of the fortress.

The Lachish Letters

During excavations in 1935, archaeologists found eighteen letters in the gatehouse chambers at Lachish that date to the second campaign of Nebuchadnezzar II against Judah in 587 BC. Because Lachish was a defensive city protecting the way to Jerusalem from the West, the city was attacked and besieged several times by the major powers of the Ancient Near East. There are remains of an Assyrian siege ramp at Lachish that dates to Sennacherib's attack and conquest of the city in the late eighth to early seventh century BC.

The letters were directed to Ya'osh, who was a high official in Lachish, and sent by Hoshayahu, the commander of an unnamed place in the Shephelah. The letters have a tone of urgency, but the matters discussed are only alluded to. So, the contents are quite obscure.

FIGURE 2.2.9.
NenyaAleks / Wikimedia Commons. Copyright in the Public Domain.

Seal Inscriptions

Seals were widely used throughout the Iron Age. This is attested by the large quantity found and the large quantity of bullae and seal-impressions found on vessels. Bullae are small, round clay seal impressions. These seals usually contain their owner's name and the father's name in two lines, occasionally accompanied by the picture of an animal. On the few pieces belonging to royal officers, the office held is mentioned, along with the name.

Seal impressions on handles of jugs are an item unique to Judah. The handles were stamped with a seal containing the word meaning "belonging to the king," accompanied with one of four place names: Hebron, Ziph, Socho, or ממשׁת. Beside the inscription is the symbol of a winged scarab with either two or four wings. These seals are meant to mark the jugs concerned as royal property. It is thought that the vessels served in the maintenance of royal officers or troops in various parts of Judah, with the deliveries probably originating from various areas of the kingdom. The cities mentioned were probably centers of royal administration.

FIGURE 2.2.10.
Funhistory / Wikimedia Commons. Copyright in the Public Domain.

2.3   The Hebrew Alphabet (Part 2)

Now, let's turn our attention back to the Hebrew alphabet. Remember, when learning to read any language, the alphabet of that language must be memorized. Biblical Hebrew is no different. Below is the remainder of the consonantal alphabet of Biblical Hebrew that we began in Chapter 1. As before, memorize the symbol, its name, and its sound.

Hints:
- With just a couple of exceptions (silent letters), the names of the letters will tell you the sound. Lamed = l, Mem = m, Samek = s, and so on.
- Learn the alphabet in order, just like you learned the English alphabet.
- There are Aleph-Bet songs on YouTube that might help you by putting music to the alphabet. This is much like how English readers learn the English alphabet song. Simply search for the Aleph-Bet song on the Internet and choose your favorite.

Symbol	Name	Sound
ל	Lamed	l as in light
מ	Mem	m as in mom; ם = final form Mem. It will always be at the end of a word.
נ	Nun	n as in noon; ן = final form Nun. It will always be at the end of a word.
ס	Samek	s as in sister
ע	Ayin	Silent
פ	Pe	p as in pop; ף = final form Pe. It will always be at the end of a word.
צ	Tsade	ts as in cats; ץ = final form Tsade. It will always be at the end of a word.
ק	Qof	k as in king
ר	Resh	r as in roar

Symbol	Name	Sound
שׂ	Sin	s as in <u>s</u>ister
שׁ	Shin	sh as in <u>sh</u>ip
ת	Tav	t as in <u>t</u>o<u>t</u>

2.4 Writing Block Letters

Your handwriting of Biblical Hebrew will not look like the printed fonts you will be seeing in print. Yours will most likely be blockier. But, strive to be clear and precise. Be careful to make each letter distinct. Take care not to make letters look alike.

2.5 Exercises

Writing Space Be careful and precise	Letter Name	Hebrew Consonant
		ל
		מ
		נ
		ס
		ע
		פ
		צ
		ק
		ר
		שׁ
		שׂ
		ת

1. Practice writing the letters. Remember, Hebrew is written and read from right to left. So practice writing the letters beginning on the right side of the provided space. Write each letter enough times to become proficient. If the space provided is not enough, use your own lined paper to practice.

2. Which inscription is the oldest ever found in Jerusalem?

_____

3. Which king of Israel is mentioned in the Tel Dan inscription?

_____

4. Which inscription reveals farming details?

_____

5. What is another name for the City of David south of the Temple Mount in Jerusalem?

_____

6. What is the time/age called that spans the years 1200 to 586 BC, and roughly corresponds with the rise of biblical Israel?

_____

7. In what biblical city was the Goliath inscription found?

_____

8. Hezekiah's tunnel connects which two bodies of water?

_____

2.6 Further Reading

Arnold, Bill T., and Bryan E. Beyer. 2002. *Readings from the Ancient Near East: Primary Sources for Old Testament Studies.* Encountering Biblical Studies. Walter A. Elwell, Series General Editor. Grand Rapids, MI: Baker.

Mazar, Eilat. "Earliest Alphabetical Inscription Found in Jerusalem." http://www.keytodavidscity.com/earliest-alphabetical-inscription-found-in-jerusalem-3/.

Roden, Chet. "David and Goliath," "Sennacherib," "The House of David," "The Moabite Stone," "Hezekiah's Tunnel," and "The Merneptah Stele." *I-tunes U.* Liberty University, Seminary, Old Testament 502, Biblical Archaeology. January to May, 2010.

Rollston, Christopher. 2010. *Writing and Literacy in the World of Ancient Israel.* Atlanta, GA: Society of Biblical Literature.

Shanks, Hershel. 2010. "Prize Find: Oldest Hebrew Inscription." *Biblical Archaeology Review* March/April: 51–54.

Tov, Emanuel. 1992. *Textual Criticism of the Hebrew Bible.* Minneapolis, MN: Fortress Press.

Vowels

3.1 Learning the Hebrew Vowels

As mentioned in Chapter 2, the Hebrew text we have today was not standardized until very recently, compared to how long the Hebrew Bible has been in existence. Vowels or vowel pointings were the latest addition to the Hebrew text, meaning the consonantal text is much more ancient than the vocalized version of the text. Further, it should be noted that the consonantal foundation of the Masoretic text has been the authoritative text since the second century AD, whereas the vocalization is still often debated today. So, you will find in some commentaries that scholars focus on the consonantal texts rather than the Masoretic text when attempting to bring clarity to words or phrases.

To ensure clarity and proper understanding of words, the vowels were added. Therefore, students of the Hebrew language must learn the vowel systems and how they work within the consonants, to bring clarity and standardization of meaning to the text.

The first stage of vocalization was the addition of consonantal letters called *matres lectionis*, which literally means "mothers of reading." The letters י, ו, and ה were added to words to indicate long final vowels. Later on, the matres lectionis were added to indicate middle vowels of words as well. The system worked fine but was applied in an irregular manner. Not all words that needed matres lectionis were given them. Furthermore, some words would have the matres lectionis in some passages but not in others. As a result, grammarians will point out two types of spellings: *full* and *defective*. Full spelling refers to the words that have one or more matres lectionis added, whereas defective spelling refers to the words that do not have the matres lectionis, even when they are appropriate.

As you can see from this brief introduction, the vocalization of the Hebrew text is somewhat complicated. At the end of the chapter there are several references to which you can turn if you are interested in a detailed history of the vocalization of the text.

3.1.1 Simple Vowels

Since the vowels were added to the consonantal text in order to preserve it, the Masoretes devised a system called "vowel pointing," which mostly works around the consonants. Vowels are primarily below the consonants, but also to the left and above the consonants. For our demonstration purposes, we will use the consonant ב as a constant for demonstrating vowels and how they work. You will see vowels placed below it, to the left of it, and above it.

Remember, Hebrew is read from right to left. But also keep in mind that as you are reading right to left, with just a few exceptions, consonants are pronounced first, then the vowel.

There are two more features of vowels with which you should be acquainted. 1) Vowels are categorized as long or short. Long vowel are those that can never be shortened. They are also called "unchangeably" long. Short vowels can be changed. More will be discussed about long and short vowels in the discussion about syllables. 2) Vowels are also classified into "A class," "E class," and "O class." These classifications are based upon the sound qualities of the vowel. For the purposes of this text, we will simply classify the vowels as Simple Vowels, Vowel Letters, and Reduced Vowels.

The Pathach

The first vowel to memorize is the Pathach (-). The older pronunciation is as the "a" in "cat" or "path." The more modern pronunciation is like an "a" in "father." So you may hear it both ways. By remembering the name of the letter, Pathach, the pronunciation is easier to remember as the "a in path." The Pathach is a short horizontal line (like a path) underneath a consonant: בַּ

Remember that you should pronounce the Bet first, then the Pathach.

The Qamets

The second vowel to memorize is the Qamets (ָ). The Qamets is pronounced like the "a" in "car" and "father." The letter "a" in the name Qamets is pronounced that way, too. Like the Pathach, the Qamets is positioned underneath the consonant: בָּ

The Bet is pronounced first, then the Qamets. The Qamets has a twin called a Qamets Hatuf. The Qamets Hatuf looks identical but is pronounced like the "o" in "hole." We will address it later.

The Hireq

The third simple vowel to remember is the Hireq (ִ). The Hireq is pronounced like the "i" in "hit." When you say the name Hireq, you would pronounce the "i" as you would in "hit." The Hireq is a single dot underneath the consonant: בִ

The Bet is pronounced first, then the Hireq.

The Tsere

The Tsere (ֵ) is the fourth simple vowel to remember, and should be pronounced as the "e" in "they." The "Ts" in the name should be pronounced like the "ts" in "hats." The "e" in Tsere should be pronounced like the "e" in "they." Like the previous simple vowels, the Tsere is placed below the consonant and will look like this: בֵ

The Bet is pronounced first, then the Tsere.

The Seghol

The fifth simple vowel is the Seghol. The Seghol is a triangle or pyramid of dots (ֶ). The Seghol is an "e" sound as in "bet" and "set." In the name Seghol, pronounce the "e" the same way. It too is written underneath the consonant: בֶ

The Bet is pronounced first, then the Seghol.

The Qibbuts

The sixth simple vowel is the Qibbuts. The Qibbuts is a diagonal line of dots (ֻ). The Qibbuts is pronounced like the "u" in "pull." The "Q" in the name Qibbuts is pronounced like a "k" or hard "c." The Qibbuts is also written beneath the consonant and will look like this: בֻ

The Bet is pronounced first, and then the Qibbuts.

The Holem

The seventh simple vowel is the Holem (ֹ). The Holem is a long "o" sound as in the word "hole." The name is pronounced the same way. The Holem is unlike the previous simple vowels in that it is written above and to the left of the consonant with which it is pronounced: בֹ

As has been the case with the other vowels thus far, the Bet is pronounced first, then the Holem.

When the Holem is paired with a consonant that precedes a שׁ, the Holem will often assimilate with the dot of the שׁ like in the word מֹשֶׁה = *Moses* (pronounced Mō/shé). The Holem has assimilated with the dot above the שׁ. Sometimes the Holem will appear with the שׁ as two dots, but usually it will be assimilated.

The Qamets Hatuf

The Qamets Hatuf is the twin of the Qamets. They look identical inside a word, but are pronounced differently. The Qamets Hatuf (ָ) is pronounced like the long "o" of the Holem, like the "o" in "hole." The difference in sound between the Qamets and Qamets Hatuf is due to how syllabification of Hebrew words works, and we will briefly discuss that later. For now, just note that there is Qamets and a Qamets Hatuf, which look the same but sound different. In the vast majority of cases, the vowel will be the Qamets and should be pronounced like the "a" as in "father."

Summary of Simple Vowels

So, there are eight simple vowels. Study and know them. The chart below should be memorized.

Symbol	Vowel Name	Sound	Symbol with בּ
ַ	Pathach	"a" as in "p**a**th"	בַּ
ָ	Qamets	"a" as in "f**a**ther"	בָּ
ִ	Hireq	"i" as in "h**i**t"	בִּ
ֵ	Tsere	"e" as in "th**ey**"	בֵּ
ֶ	Seghol	"e" as in "s**e**t"	בֶּ
ֻ	Qibbuts	"u" as in "p**u**ll"	בֻּ
ֹ	Holem	"o" as in "h**o**le"	בֹּ
ָ	Qamets Hatuf	"o" as in "h**o**le"	בָּ

3.1.2 Vowel Letters

The vowels were first introduced into the consonantal text through the usage of vowel letters. The vowel letters are י, ו, and ה. These are the matres lectionis discussed earlier. These consonants were added to indicate vowel sounds in words. Later, when the vowel points were added, simple vowels were added to these letters, and thus they became vowel letters. There are nine of these vowel letters. In each case, a simple vowel and one of these three consonants combine to make a single vowel. They are not to be seen as a consonant and a vowel, but one vowel. So, remember, the vowel letters are two symbols combined into a single vowel unit. With the exception of the Shureq, their names are indicative of the combination of symbols into one sound. Plus, the names are simply the names of the two combining symbols. The chart below should also be memorized.

Symbol	Vowel Name	Sound	Symbol with ב
ִי	Hireq Yod	"i" as in "mach**i**ne"	בִּי
ֵי	Tsere Yod	"e" as in "th**ey**"	בֵּי
ֶי	Seghol Yod	"e" as in "s**e**t"	בֶּי
וֹ	Holem Waw/Vav	"o" as in "h**o**le"	בּוֹ
וּ	Shureq	"u" as in "r**u**le"	בּוּ
ָה	Qamets He	"a" as in "f**a**ther"	בָּה
ֵה	Tsere He	"e" as in "th**ey**"	בֵּה
ֶה	Seghol He	"e" as in "s**e**t"	בֶּה
ֹה	Holem He	"o" as in "h**o**le"	בֹּה

3.1.3 Reduced Vowels and the Sheva

Reduced vowels are vowels with a hurried or rushed sound. They are simple vowel symbols that are combined with a Sheva (ְ). The reduced vowels and Sheva are written below the consonant.

There are two types of Sheva: a vocal Sheva and a silent Sheva. The vocal Sheva is always pronounced and is the one that combines with the simple vowels to make reduced vowels. The silent Sheva is a syllable indicator inside a word and is never pronounced. More about the silent Sheva will be discussed in the section on syllabification.

The pronunciation of the reduced vowels is a hurried sound. Say aloud the words, "because, align, mechanic, and today." Notice how quickly you say the first sounds. While each of the distinctive vowel sounds are there, when pronounced, the sounds almost come out like "buh," "uh," "muh," and "tuh." The emphasis is not on the sound quality so much as it is the brevity of sound. The reduced vowels display the vowel sound quality, and when combined with the Sheva also indicate the brevity of sound. One more characteristic of the reduced vowels should be noted. The Hateph Qamets always takes on the "o" sound of the Qamets Hatuf and never the "a" sound of the Qamets. Review and memorize the chart below.

Symbol	Vowel Name	Sound	Symbol with ב
ְ	Sheva	"e" in "b**e**cause"	בְּ
ֲ	Hateph Pathach	"a" as in "**a**lign"	בֲּ
ֱ	Hateph Seghol	"e" as in "m**e**chanic"	בֱּ
ֳ	Hateph Qamets	"o" like "t**o**day"	בֳּ

3.1.4 Reading Words

Now that we have the consonants and the vowels, reading can begin. Below are some simple, one-syllable words that appear very frequently in the Hebrew Bible. Keep these three rules in mind as you attempt to read the words:

1. Read from the right to left.

2. Pronounce the words by pronouncing the consonant first then its accompanying vowel.

3. If the consonant is silent (א, ע), simply pronounce the accompanying vowel.

Reading Example:

כֹּל = should be read כ + ֹ + ל. The word is pronounced "cōl" and means *all, each, every*. Note that the Holem is pronounced as an "o" in "hole."

מִן = should be read מ + ִ + ן. The word is pronounced "min" and means *from, out of*. Note that the last consonant is a Final Nun.

Single Syllable Vocabulary:

מִן = *from, out of*

כֹּל also spelled כּוֹל = *all, each, every* (note the Holem Vav and the full spelling)

אֶל = *unto, toward* (the Aleph is silent)

אֵת = *with, beside*

בּוֹא = *go in, enter, come*

בֵּן = *son*

יוֹם = *day* (note the Final Mem is the last consonant)

כִּי = *because, for, that, when, but; indeed, truly* (note the vowel is a Hireq Yod)

עַל = *on, upon, against, over* (the Ayin is silent)

אָב = *father*

אִם = *if, then*

יָד = *hand*

אִישׁ = *man*

הוּא = *he*

הִיא = *she*

שׁוּב = *to turn back, return, go/come back*

מוּת = *to die*

קוּם = *to rise, arise, get up, stand up*

שִׂים = *to establish, to set up, to put, place, lay, confirm*

סוּר = *to turn aside, turn off, leave off*

3.2 The Dagesh

3.2.1 Dagesh Lene and the *BeGaD KePhaT* Letters

While learning the alphabet, you may have noticed that some letters had a dot in the middle of them, namely the letters תפכ דגב. These six letters have come to be known as the *BeGaD KePhaT* letters. That term is simply a device to help you remember the letters that have that dot. The dot is called a Dagesh Lene. The Dagesh Lene is only found in the *BeGaD KePhaT* letters. The Dagesh Lene changes the pronunciation of these six letters and reveals how the letters are supposed to be pronounced. In Modern Hebrew, only three of these letters (פכב) have an obviously different pronunciation. Some textbooks use the Biblical pronunciations, in which the Dagesh Lene changes all six of the pronunciations to the hard sound. For our purposes, the three major changes acknowledged in the Modern Hebrew will be sufficient. Review and learn the chart below.

THE *BeGaD KePhaT* LETTERS

בּ = b as in boy   ב = v as in vine
גּ = g as in give   ג = g as in give
דּ = d as in dog   ד = d as in dog
כּ = k as in king   כ = k as in koala; or ch as in loch or Bach (much throatier)
פּ = p as in pop   פ = f as in face
תּ = t as in tot   ת = t as in tot

3.2.2 Dagesh Forte

Like the Dagesh Lene, the Dagesh Forte is a dot that occurs in consonants. The purpose of the Dagesh Forte is to indicate a doubling of the consonant for syllabification purposes. Rather than writing a consonant twice, the Dagesh Forte was added. The trouble for readers is deciding which Dagesh is being used, the Lene or Forte. Below are some rules to determine which Dagesh it is. These need to be studied and learned.

1. If the consonant is **NOT** a *BeGaD KePhaT* letter, then the dot is a Dagesh Forte.

2. If the consonant is a *BeGaD KePhaT* letter, the dot can either be Dagesh Lene or Forte. Three options help determine which it is:

   a. If at the beginning of a word, it is a Dagesh Lene.
   c. If immediately following a silent Sheva, it is a Dagesh Lene.
   d. If immediately following a vowel, it is a Dagesh Forte.

Note: In the *BeGaD KePhaT* letters, the Dagesh Forte also acts like a Lene concerning pronunciation. It will double the consonant and harden the pronunciation of that consonant.

3.3 The Gutturals

The letters א, ע, ה, ח, and ר are called "gutturals" because they are pronounced in the back regions of the throat. In modern times, the א and ע have become basically silent. Originally, they were pronounced with varying distinctions of the sound your throat makes just as you begin to say "uh oh." It is that deep throaty sound. Today, most will count them as silent and simply pronounce the vowel associated with them.

The ה and the ח have similar "h" sounds, but with a differing harshness to the sound. The ה is a throaty "h" sound. Say aloud the words "hit" and "hot." The ה is more like the "h" in "hot." The ח is a much harsher "h" sound which originates deep in the throat, similar to clearing the throat. Pronounce the word "loch" and "Bach." That deep final sound of those words is the sound of the ח.

The ר often acts like a guttural as well. The pronunciation of the ר is the rolled "r" sound found in Spanish, but with a trill deeper in the throat. The characteristics that define the usage of gutturals will quite often govern the ר as well.

3.3.1 Governing Characteristics of Gutturals

1. Gutturals prefer "a class" vowels, particularly the Pathach.

2. Gutturals take Hateph Shevas instead of a vocal Sheva. Most often it will be the Hateph Pathach (-:).

3. Gutturals reject the Dagesh Forte, thus cannot be doubled.

3.4 Exercises

1. On a separate piece of paper, write out the eight simple vowels using a Bet, like this: בַּ בָּ בְּ בִּ בֵּ בֶּ בֹּ בֻּ

2. On a separate piece of paper, write out the nine vowel letters using a Bet, as in exercise 1.

3. On a separate piece of paper, write out the Sheva and the three reduced vowels, using a Bet as in exercise 1.

4. On a separate piece of paper, write out all the single syllable vocabulary words, along with their meanings. Afterward, cover the meanings and memorize the vocabulary list.

5. On a separate piece of paper, write out the Hebrew *BeGaD KePhaT* letters.

6. On a separate piece of paper, write the gutturals.

7. On a separate piece of paper, list the governing characteristics of the gutturals.

8. Using the Dagesh rules above (3.2.2), determine whether the Dagesh in the words below are Dagesh Lene or Dagesh Forte.

   a. כֹּל

   b. בֵּן

   c. הִנֵּה

   d. מָוֶת

   e. גַּם

   f. אַתָּה

   g. מִשְׁפָּת

3.5 Further Reading

Brotzman, Ellis R. 1994. *Old Testament Textual Criticism: A Practical Introduction*. Grand Rapids, MI: Baker.

Tov, Emanuel. 2011. *Textual Criticism of the Hebrew Bible*, third edition revised and expanded. Minneapolis, MN: Fortress.

Würthwein, Ernst. 2014. *The Text of the Old Testament: An Introduction to the Biblica Hebraica*, third edition. Revised and expanded by Alexander Achilles Fischer. Translated by Erroll F. Rhodes. Grand Rapids, MI: Eerdmans.

Chapter 4: Nouns, Syllabification, Accents, and Reading

4.1 Hebrew Nouns

As in English, to put things simply, nouns are people, places, and things. To be more grammatically specific, however, nouns are words that act as the subjects and objects in sentences. For instance, consider the sentence *Thomas plowed the field*. *Thomas* is the subject and is a noun. *Field* is also a noun and is the direct object. Both are within the category of person, place, or thing. The same rule applies in Hebrew. Nouns are people, places, or things.

Hebrew nouns have five distinct attributes that you must memorize. Hebrew nouns can be

1. singular: just one

2. plural: more than one

3. dual: things that most often come in pairs—two eyes, two ears, and so on. But the duality can simply indicate two things, such as two horses, two apples, two words.

4. masculine in gender

5. feminine in gender

To mark the attributes above, Hebrew uses suffixes that attach to nouns. Since we read Hebrew from the right to the left, suffixes are attached to the left of words (Suffix←Noun). For example, let's use the word סוּס (*horse*), whose root word is masculine.

Example:

	Singular	**Plural**
Masculine	סוּס horse	סוּסִים horses

Notice that in the masculine singular (ms), there is nothing added. But in the masculine plural (mp), the ִים has been added. In their root forms, nouns are classified as either masculine or feminine. So, in this case the root of סוּס is the ms form.

Below are the feminine suffixes.

Example:

	Singular	**Plural**
Feminine	סוּסָה mare	סוּסוֹת mares

In the feminine, there are suffixes added to both the feminine singular (fs) and the feminine plural (fp). For the fs, the ָה suffix has been added to סוּס to show it is a female horse, or a mare. In the fp case, the וֹת suffix has been added. You'll also need to note that there are three different suffixes for the fs: ָה, ַת, and וֹת.

The dual suffix, which indicates two of something, is ַיִם and is used in both masculine and feminine forms. **Dual** = סוּסַיִם = *two horses, a pair of horses.*

The chart below should be memorized.

	Singular	**Plural**
Masculine	סוּס horse	סוּסִים horses
Feminine	סוּסָה mare	סוּסוֹת mares
Dual		סוּסַיִם two horses

4.2 Syllabification

The syllable in Biblical Hebrew begins with a consonant and contains one full vowel, which together create one sound. The word כִּי is spoken by pronouncing the Kaph and then the vowel Hireq Yod to make the sound "key." In this sample, there is one consonant כ and one vowel ִי. This sample is known as an open syllable. Open syllables contain a consonant and a corresponding vowel. Sometimes, a consonant with a reduced vowel will begin the syllable. But the reduced vowel does not constitute a syllable. That reduced vowel sound becomes part of the following syllable. A syllable must have just one full vowel.

The other type of syllable is a closed syllable. Closed syllables begin with a consonant, contain a corresponding full vowel, and close with another consonant. Most of the vocabulary in Chapter 3 consists of closed, one-syllable words. The words שׁוּב = *to turn back, return, go/come back*; מוּת = *to die*; and קוּם = *to rise, arise, get up, stand up* are examples of closed syllables. They all begin with a consonant, contain a corresponding full vowel, and close with a consonant.

You will need to pay attention to those words that end with the aleph (א) and the he (ה). The words הוּא = *he*, הִיא = *she*, זֶה = *this*, and פֶּה = *mouth* look like they are closed syllables, but are considered open. The confusion arises because the aleph and the he are silent and lose their consonantal qualities. This type of syllable should be understood as opened.

As is the case with any language, there are exceptions to all of these generalizations. But since you are just beginning to understand the language, learn the generalities and then progress into the exceptions and finer details. Memorize the following guidelines about syllables.

1. Syllables begin with a consonant.

2. Syllables must contain one full vowel.

3. Open syllables end with a vowel or with an א or ה.

4. Closed syllables begin and end with a consonant and contain one full vowel.

4.3   Accents and Special Marks

When we speak, we accent words without even thinking about it. Say aloud the word "examine." As we speak it, the syllable "a" is the accented syllable. It receives the thrust of the vocalization. Try saying it while emphasizing the "ex" syllable. That just doesn't work very well and doesn't sound right. Say aloud the word "review." The syllable "view" gets most of the emphasis, while the "re" syllable is said quickly and without emphasis. We are placing the accent on the words without realizing it. Now say aloud the word "rewind." Where did you place the accent/emphasis? Most of us say "RE-wind." English accents are all over the place and vary from region to region of the spoken language. Hebrew accents are easier.

Accents in Biblical Hebrew are much more consistent and the accented syllable is usually indicated in modern print. The Masoretes, who vocalized the texts, also wanted the reader to be able correctly pronounce and chant the words in public settings. So, they added accents throughout the text. The accented syllable in each word is called the "tone" or "tonic" syllable. Unless specified, the tone will be the last syllable of a word. For instance, the word דָּבָר = *word, thing* has two syllables. The first syllable דָּ is an open syllable pronounced "dah." The second syllable בָר (pronounced "var") is a closed syllable and the last syllable. Since there are no other accent markings in the word and בָר is the last syllable, it becomes the tonic syllable receiving the most emphasis. So, דָּבָר is pronounced "dah-VAR," with a slight vocal emphasis on the last syllable.

If the tone syllable is somewhere else in the word, the text will indicate where the accent should be. The most notable accent mark, and the one with which we will mainly concern ourselves, is the < symbol above the tonic syllable. For example, the words מֶלֶךְ = *king, ruler* and אֶרֶץ = *land, earth* are accented on the first syllable with the <. Thus, that first syllable becomes the tonic syllable and should be pronounced with emphasis. The word מֶלֶךְ should be pronounced "MEH-lek" with a slight emphasis on the "meh." Likewise with אֶרֶץ. The tonic syllable is the first syllable and receives the emphasis.

In other cases, the tonic is in the middle of words. The word שָׁמַיִם = *heavens or sky* has an accent on the middle syllable. The first syllable שָׁ is an open, unaccented syllable. Since it is just prior to the tonic syllable, it is called the pre-tonic syllable. The second syllable מַ is an open, accented syllable and is the tonic syllable. Since it is the tonic syllable, it receives the emphasis of pronunciation. The last syllable יִם is a closed, unaccented syllable. Thus, the word שָׁמַיִם is pronounced "sha-MA-yim," with a slight vocal emphasis on the "ma." Again, the tonic syllable is מַ and the pre-tonic is שָׁ.

Soph Pasuq

The Soph Pasuq (׃) is another accent mark that should be noted at this stage of your learning. The Soph Pasuq will indicate the end of a verse and is important for indicating the verses and chapters. You will see this throughout the Hebrew texts at the end of verses.

Example:
(Gen. 1:1) בְּרֵאשִׁית בָּרָא אֱלֹהִים אֵת הַשָּׁמַיִם וְאֵת הָאָרֶץ׃
(Ps. 2:11) עִבְדוּ אֶת־יְהוָה בְּיִרְאָה וְגִילוּ בִּרְעָדָה׃

Maqqef

The Maqqef is a horizontal stroke (-) that connects two words together, as in the example above from Psalms 2:11 אֶת־יְהוָה. The Maqqef typically joins one-syllable (monosyllabic) words to other words, and the two words function as one. The accent will be focused on the last word.

The Furtive Pathach

As you learned in Chapter 3, the Pathach is a short horizontal line underneath a consonant: בַּ. It is pronounced like the "a" in "path." In normal settings, you should pronounce the consonant first, then the Pathach.

The Furtive Pathach is a short horizontal line like the Pathach and is pronounced the same way. The difference between them is where the Furtive Pathach occurs in a word, the position of how it is written under the consonant, and when it is pronounced. Let's look at an example.

The Furtive Pathach occurs at the end of a word that ends with ה or ע. One of the more well-known words using the Furtive Pathach is רוּחַ = *spirit, wind*. The vowel accompanying the ח is the Furtive Pathach. Notice its position under the consonant. It is written under the right leg of the ח. That position helps us know to pronounce it *before* the consonant ח. So the word is pronounced "ru-ach" (remember the ח is pronounced like the "ch" in Bach).

To summarize, the Furtive Pathach is found in words ending with ה or ע, is positioned underneath the right side of those consonants, and is pronounced *before* those consonants.

Mappiq

The Mappiq is another special mark that occurs at the end of a word. Typically, when a word ends with the letter ה, the ה is silent. In some instances, when the ה ends a word, it is supposed to be pronounced. When it is to retain its sound, it will occur with a dot in the middle that looks like the Dagesh הּ. This dot is known as the Mappiq.

4.4 Reading Hebrew

One of the more confusing aspects of Biblical Hebrew for first-time language students is getting adjusted to the word order of Hebrew sentences. In English, the typical order for simple sentences is Subject, Verb, Object. *The girl drove the car* is a good example of this type of word order. The subject is "the girl." The verb is "drove" and the object is "the car."

Hebrew word order is different. Typical word order is Verb, Subject, Object. Writers will regularly emphasize the subject by placing it first in the sentence, like in the English order. But that is for emphasis, and is not the regular pattern. Here is the Hebrew word order: *She drove the girl the car*. In this type of order, the emphasis is on the action. Thus, verbs and understanding them are very important to the Biblical Hebrew language. In Hebrew grammars this can be seen very clearly. It is typical that the verbal system will occupy well over half of the teaching in the text. We will not follow that pattern in this elementary grammar. We will instead give an overview the verb system as a whole, but delve only into verbal stems and their usage.

At this juncture, know and understand the following characteristics of reading Hebrew words and sentences.

1. Read the words and sentences from the right to the left (←←Start).

2. Pronounce the consonant first, then the accompanying vowel, then the closing consonant if in a closed syllable (C←V←C).

3. Read the sentences beginning at the top right of the page, moving toward the left, progressing line-by-line toward the bottom left (⇐).

4. Normal word order for Hebrew sentences is Object←Subject←Verb.

4.5 Basic Vocabulary

Take a look at the vocabulary below. These are some of the most-used nouns in the Hebrew Bible. These should be memorized, along with those in Chapter 3, before completing the exercises.

אֱלֹהִים = *God or gods*

מֶלֶךְ = *king, ruler*

אֶרֶץ = *land, earth*

אִשָּׁה = *woman*

פָּנִים = *face, in front of, front*

בַּ֫יִת	= house
עִיר	= city
דָּבָר	= word, thing
עַ֫יִן	= eye, spring
אֲנִי	= I (personal pronoun)
ר֫וּחַ	= spirit, wind
שָׁמַ֫יִם	= heavens, sky

4.6 Exercises

1. Name the five distinct attributes of Hebrew nouns.

2. Without help, attempt to write the noun chart with ms, mp, fs, fp, and dual endings from section 4.1.

3. What are the two types of syllables? What is the difference between them?

4. What is the accented syllable of a word called?

5. Name the syllable that precedes the accented syllable.

6. Which special mark indicates the end of a verse?

7. The horizontal line that connects two word together as one unit is called what?

_____

8. Write out the typical word order for English sentences. Write the typical word order for Hebrew sentences.

_____

9. The simple sentences below are constructed from the vocabulary in Chapters 3 and 4. Make sure you know most of them from memory. Try to translate the sentences from memory as best you can. For now, translate the verbs in the past tense. For instance, the word בּוֹא = *go in, enter, come* should be translated "went in, entered, came." If these are a struggle for you, don't worry just yet. The answers are provided. But try to work through each Hebrew sentence before looking at the answers.

_____

← ← ← ← ← ← Remember to read from right to left.

10. בּוֹא אִישׁ   Answer: A man went in/entered/or came

_____

_____

11. מוּת אָב   Answer: A father died

_____

_____

1. שִׂים אֱלֹהִים מֶלֶךְ   Answer: God established a king

_____

_____

m. סוּר הוּא   Answer: He turned aside

n. שׁוּב אִישׁ מִן בַּיִת   Answer: A man returned from a house

o. קוּם רוּחַ אֶל שָׁמַיִם   Answer: A spirit rose to heaven/the sky

4.7 Further Reading

Fuller, Russell T., and Kyoungwon Choi. 2006. *Invitation to Biblical Hebrew: A Beginning Grammar*. Grand Rapids. MI: Kregel.

Garrett, Duane A., and Jason S. DeRouchie. 2009. *A Modern Grammar for Biblical Hebrew*. Nashville, TN: B&H Academic.

Kelley, Page H. 1992. *Biblical Hebrew: An Introductory Grammar*. Grand Rapids, MI: Eerdmans.

Pratico, Gary D., and Miles V. Van Pelt. 2007. *Basics of Biblical Hebrew*, second edition. Grand Rapids, MI: Zondervan.

Van Pelt, Miles V. 2010. *English Grammar to ACE Biblical Hebrew*. Grand Rapids, MI: Zondervan.

Chapter 5

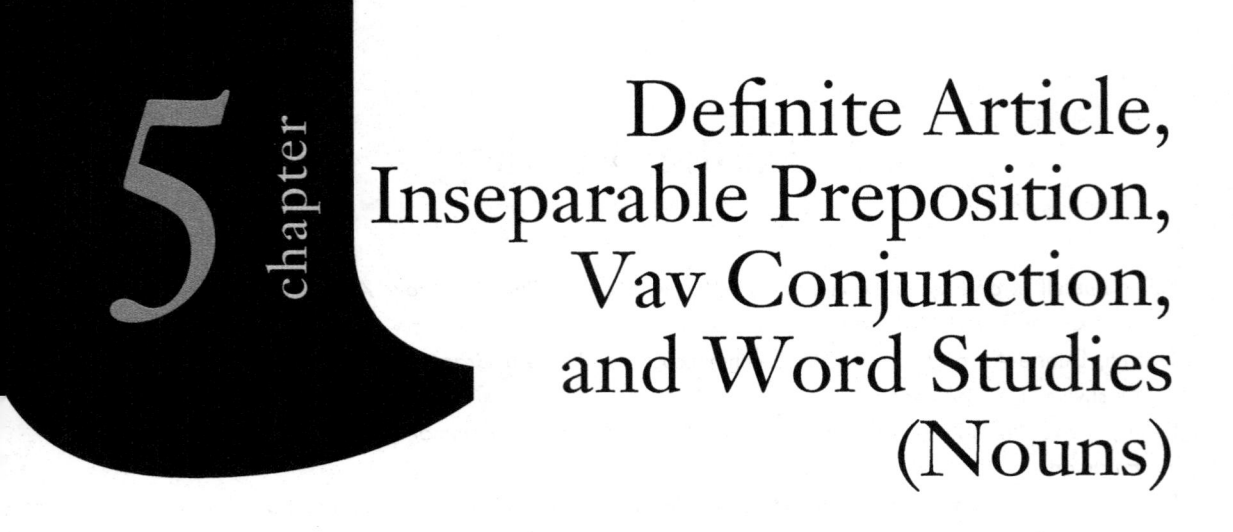

Definite Article, Inseparable Preposition, Vav Conjunction, and Word Studies (Nouns)

5.1 Definite Article

In language, there are a few ways to specify which particular person, place, thing, or idea is being described in a sentence. One of the primary ways is to use a definite article. In English, "the" is the definite article. By using "the" instead of "a," the specificity increases, going from "a noun" (one among many), to "the noun" (one specifically). In English we use the word "the," and it is a separate word from the noun it is identifying. Instead of using a separate, distinct word, Hebrew attaches a prefix to a noun (Noun←Prefix) to indicate definiteness. Since there is no indefinite article ("a" noun) in Hebrew, nouns without the definite article prefix are considered indefinite unless other grammar rules dictate otherwise.

The Hebrew definite article prefix is made up of three elements: the consonant ה, the accompanying vowel Pathach (ַ), and a Dagesh Forte in the first letter of the noun.

Example:

NOUN	←	Definite Article
מֶלֶךְ	←	הַ ּ = הַמֶּלֶךְ
a king	the	= the king

There are some situations that deviate from the typical definite article shown above. As we work through those deviations below, you will want to note the constancy of the ה. It should become one of the major keys you use to identify the definite article. The consistency of the ה must not become the only thing you look for, however. You will learn that when inseparable prepositions are added to a definite noun, the ה will disappear. But we will point that out later and give you the tools to identify when that happens.

The most obvious changes in the definite article are those arising from the Dagesh Forte, which is inserted into the first letter of the noun. You have learned already that the gutturals cannot take a Dagesh Forte. So, if a noun begins with a guttural or Resh, and has the definite article, there are some vowel changes that happen to the Pathach of the definite article because of that rejection of the Dagesh Forte. Let's look at these reactions.

The first reaction is called *compensatory lengthening*. Compensatory lengthening happens in the definite article with nouns that begin with the gutturals א, ר, and ע. In these definite nouns, the Pathach lengthens to become a Qamets (ָ). Thus the definite article would look like the examples below.

Examples:

Noun	With Definite Article	
רוּחַ	הָרוּחַ	= the spirit
עִיר	הָעִיר	= the city
אֶרֶץ	הָאָרֶץ	= the earth, land

In these examples above, the initial consonant of the noun has rejected the Dagesh of the definite article, causing the definite article Pathach to lengthen to a Qamets.

The second reaction is called *virtual doubling*. Virtual doubling occurs when a noun begins with the ה and ח, and takes the definite article. In this situation, these gutturals reject the Dagesh Forte, but the Pathach is not lengthened. It remains a Pathach. It is virtually doubled. Consider the examples below.

Examples:

Noun		With Definite Article	
הַר	= hill, mountain	הַהַר	= the hill, mountain
חֶסֶד	= mercy, loyalty	הַחֶסֶד	= the mercy, loyalty

A third reaction we must mention is that, for a certain collection of nouns that begin with a guttural, the first vowel of the noun will lengthen to a Qamets (ָ). You may have noticed it in two of the above examples. We have included them below to highlight the change. Keep in mind that there are several of these nouns whose first letter changes to a Qamets. The examples below simply show the pattern of change.

Examples:

Noun	**With Definite Article**
הַר = hill, mountain	הָהָר = the hill, mountain
אֶרֶץ = earth, land	הָאָרֶץ = the earth, land

A fourth reaction to the definite article occurs when the noun begins with an unaccented עָ, הָ, or חָ. In these three cases, the vowel of the definite article changes to a Seghol (ֶ).

Example:

חָכָם = wise man becomes הֶחָכָם = the wise man

Notice there is no accent on the initial consonant of the noun, which has a Qamets as the accompanying vowel. Thus, the vowel of the definite article changes to a Seghol.

The last reaction is when the definite article occurs with a noun whose first letter is a Yod or Mem, followed by a simple Sheva (יְ מְ). In these situations, the Dagesh is rejected but the definite article vowel remains a Pathach. There are a few exceptions to this reaction in which the mem does take the Dagesh. But generally, the Dagesh is not accepted.

Example:

יְלָדִים = children becomes הַיְלָדִים = the children

Summary of the Definite Article:

1. Typical — הַמֶּלֶךְ
2. Compensatory lengthening — הָרוּחַ
3. Virtual doubling — הַחֶסֶד
4. First vowel change — הָאָרֶץ
5. Unaccented עָ, הָ, or חָ — הֶחָכָם
6. With יְ or מְ — הַיְלָדִים

5.2 Inseparable Prepositions: לְ כְּ בְּ

Prepositions are words that join words and clauses to form a closer functionality between them. Consider the phrases, "a man sat" and "a branch of the tree." In order to connect these two in a close functionality, you would use a preposition: "A man sat *upon* a branch of the tree." In this sentence, the word *upon* connects the two phrases and reveals how the two parts work together. Contemplate the difference in this preposition: "A man sat *under* a branch of the tree." The change of preposition to *under* still connects the two clauses but changes the meaning of the sentence once the two clauses are joined. Some of the most used prepositions are *in, on, by, to, for, like,* and *as*.

Hebrew prepositions function similarly in that they join words and clauses into one closely functional sentence. Some Hebrew prepositions, like English ones, are independent words (see vocabulary in Chapter 3). But, there are three widely used prepositions called inseparable prepositions. Inseparable prepositions are attached, inseparably, to the beginning of nouns. Those inseparable prepositions are בְּ, כְּ, and לְ. Each of these have an individual meaning:

בְּ = *in, with, by*

כְּ = *according to, like, as*

לְ = *to, for*

Study how these look when added to the word מֶלֶךְ below.

Example:

| NOUN | ← | Inseparable Preposition |

מֶלֶךְ ← בְּ = בְּמֶלֶךְ
a king   in/with/by = in/with/by a king

מֶלֶךְ ← כְּ = כְּמֶלֶךְ
a king   according to/like = according to/like a king

מֶלֶךְ ← לְ = לְמֶלֶךְ
a king   to/for = to/for a king

You will soon realize, if you haven't already, that there are typically exceptions to almost every rule in language. The same is true for the inseparable prepositions. The vocal Sheva of the inseparable preposition will change under the circumstances below.

If the first vowel of the noun is a reduced vowel, the vocal Sheva of the inseparable preposition will take on the short vowel of that noun's reduced vowel. Study the examples below.

Examples:

אֲרוֹן ← בְּ = בַּאֲרוֹן
an ark   in/with/by = in/with/by an ark

אֱמוּנָה ← כְּ = כֶּאֱמוּנָה
faithfulness, reliability   according to/like = according to faithfulness

Notice the vocal Shevas have changed to the corresponding short vowels of the noun's reduced vowel.

Another exception occurs with nouns beginning with a vocal Sheva. Since two vocal Shevas cannot be next to one another, the vocal Sheva of the preposition changes to a Hireq or Hireq Yod.

Example:

בִּכְלִי = בְּ ← כְּלִי
with a tool, weapon = with ← tool, weapon

5.3 Vav Conjunction

Conjunctions, like prepositions, connect words and clauses together. By far, the most widely used conjunction in Hebrew is the Vav conjunction (וְ). The most common ways the Vav conjunction is translated is *and, for, but, because, now*, and *however*. Like the inseparable prepositions, the Vav conjunction attaches as a prefix to nouns and verbs.

Example: NOUN ← Vav Conjunction

וְדָבָר = וְ ← דָּבָר
and a word, thing = and ← word, thing

Also, like the prepositions, the Sheva of the Vav conjunction will change under certain situations. Let's look at those changes. First, the Vav will become a Shureq before words beginning with ב, מ, or פ, and before nouns with a vocal Sheva.

Example: NOUN ← Vav Conjunction

וּמֶלֶךְ = וְ ← מֶלֶךְ
and a king = and ← a king

וּכְלִי = וְ ← כְּלִי
and a tool, weapon = with ← tool, weapon

Second, before nouns that begin with a י, the vocal Sheva changes to a Hireq Yod.

Example:

וִירוּשָׁלַיִם = וְ ← יְרוּשָׁלַיִם
and Jerusalem = and ← Jerusalem

Third, like inseparable prepositions, when attached to nouns that begin with a reduced vowel, the vocal Sheva of the conjunction will change to the corresponding short vowel.

Example:

אֲרוֹן	←	וְ	=	וַאֲרוֹן
an ark		and	=	and an ark
אֱמוּנָה	←	וְ	=	וֶאֱמוּנָה
faithfulness, reliability		and	=	and faithfulness

Last, the vocal Sheva of the Vav conjunction sometimes changes to a Qamets when attached to single-syllable words, and when attached to the pre-tonic syllable.

Example:

רָע	←	וְ	=	וָרָע
evil, bad, wicked		and	=	and an evil, bad, wicked

Summary of the Vav Conjunction:

1. וְ = basic
2. וּ = before words beginning with בּ, מ, or פ, and vocal Shevas
3. וִי = before nouns that begin with a יְ
4. וַ = before a reduced vowel (takes corresponding vowel)
5. וָ = before some single-syllable words and pre-tonic syllables

5.3.1 Adding Definite Articles and Inseparable Prepositions

You may have wondered how all these prefixes work together when one or more prefixes are added to the same word. The situation certainly gets crowded at the front. But there are keys to help identify each of the prefix components that attach to nouns. I have listed some ways to identify them.

1. **Look for the identifying consonants.** Each of the prefixes discussed above has distinctive consonants that are consistent throughout their usage: the prepositions בּ, כּ, and ל; the definite article ה; and the Vav conjunction ו. While the vowels change in various situations, the consonants remain (with the exception detailed in #3 below).

2. **Order is important.** When more than one prefix is attached, they follow a regular order. The Vav conjunction will always be in the first position at the beginning of the word. The inseparable prepositions will be second in order, with the definite article third.

⇐ Reading right to left
Noun←Definite Article←Vav Conjunction ⇐
Noun←Inseparable Preposition←Vav Conjunction ⇐
Noun←Definite Article←Inseparable Preposition ⇐
Noun←Definite Article←Inseparable Preposition←Vav Conjunction ⇐

3. **Find the missing consonant.** As you are looking for the identifying consonants, there will be one situation were the identifying consonant is missing. When a definite article and an inseparable preposition are both added to a noun, the ה of the definite article will disappear and be replaced by the identifying consonant of the inseparable preposition. The vowel and Dagesh of the definite article will remain and indicate the definite article. Only the ה disappears and is replaced. Study the example below.

Example:

הַמֶּלֶךְ ← לְ = מֶּלֶךְ_ = לַמֶּלֶךְ
the king   to, for = ה disappears = to, for the king

The definite article vowels remain and become the identifier of the definite article.

5.4 Word Studies: Hebrew Nouns

After having taught elementary Hebrew for years, both residentially and online, I've come to understand that doing a word study is really difficult for many people. So, I hope the following instruction will be helpful and will build your confidence. Let's begin with thoughts about why word studies are needed.

Each time a word is used, its context will help determine the word's exact meaning. Context is the setting of words, phrases, sentences, paragraphs, and chapters around any given word. While a word carries its own basic meaning, context will determine the different nuances of the word. Consider the following sentences using the same phrase: "I love."

Examples:

I love my wife.
I love my children.
I love my mother.
I love when the weather is great.
I love fruit.

Meanings:

I love my wife. This love is an emotional feeling of romance and the resulting feelings of loyalty and attachment.

I love my children. This love is an emotional feeling, too, but not a romantic feeling. This love produces attachment, pride, and a desire to nourish and cherish one's offspring.

I love my mother. This too is an emotional feeling. But it is neither romantic love nor the love felt toward children. This feeling of love is one based on appreciation, connection, and belonging.

I love when the weather is great. This emotional feeling is one of happiness based on having experienced sunshine, cool breezes, and fresh air. Those experiences produce fond, almost euphoric memories to which we attach an emotion. This love is an emotion, but not aimed at any particular being. It is produced and felt inside a person.

I love fruit. This emotion is also an emotional feeling based on experience, but also produces an anticipation as well. Because fruit tastes so good and makes our stomachs feel full and comfortable, we attach emotions to those feelings. This love is not directed to any person, but is still an emotional feeling connected to the same base of feelings as the love for a wife, children, a mother, and great weather.

So, as you can see, the contexts of the word "love" have helped define the various nuances of its meaning. The context of a word shapes the way we understand that word's meaning. We know what love means in a basic sense, but I don't love my mom or good weather the way I love my wife. The contextual nuance produces the specific understanding of the word.

What I want you to realize is that although a single Hebrew word may be used in multiple passages, there will be different English nuances for that word based on the specific context. That context is what causes translators to use different English words in an effort to clarify and expose the specific nuance dictated by the context. The nuances are what create clarity, depth, and beauty in languages. It is vital that we understand contextual nuances in order to have proper interpretations. So as you conduct a word study, continually ask, "Why does the same Hebrew word have so many English variations?"

With that in mind, the following steps are included to help you produce a word study for Hebrew nouns. There will be another set of steps for Hebrew verbs later.

Word Study Process:

1. Select only the most important words for your study.

Not every single word of a biblical text should be studied in depth. Many are so straightforward that to study them would be a counterproductive use of time. But some words are so vital to the passage that proper understanding of them is a must. But which words are the most important ones?

To decide which words to study, begin with a simple, numeric usage. If a noun is used several times in a short span, that word is probably a key to understanding that text. For instance, in Psalms 86:5–16 (12 verses), the word "mercy" is used four times, an average of once every three verses. That is frequent enough to realize "mercy" is a significant word or theme in those verses. Thus, it should be studied. In 1 Samuel 20:17, the word "loved" is used three times. Surely, such usage indicates that the word is a primary one. So, we must study what the word "loved" means in order to understand that verse. Usage is a key.

Another way of choosing which words to study is to look for the word or concept upon which the entire verse or passage centers. For instance, Genesis 13:4 says, "to the place of the altar which he had made there formerly; and there Abram called upon the name of the Lord" (New American Standard Bible; NASB). The word "altar" is the central word around which this entire verse is formed. The action begins in the phrase "to the place of the altar." Then, the explanation "which he had made there formerly" is referring to the altar. What was "made there formerly?" The altar was. "There Abram called upon the name of the Lord." Where did he call upon the Lord? He called upon the Lord at that place. What place? The place where he had built the altar! So in this verse, it would be a mistake not to understand the meaning of the word "altar" because the entire verse centers on it.

Please don't misunderstand. All words are important for sentence structure and grammatical correctness. But since time is so precious to most of us, use your time studying those words which are the most significant. Choose wisely.

2. Determine the Hebrew word from which the English word was derived.

There are several ways to do this. Today there are a number of free online Bibles and tools which will allow you to simply point and click on any English word in the Old Testament and the Hebrew word will pop up on screen. You can also determine the Hebrew behind the English by using lexicons, concordances, interlinear Bibles, word studies, and commentaries. I personally recommend the free online Bibles for this step.[13] It is the simplest and fastest way to get to the Hebrew from the English text. Once you have become proficient in Biblical Hebrew, this step will become unnecessary.

---

13 Compare these and others to see which you like best: https://www.blueletterbible.org/index.cfm; http://www.e-sword.net/; https://www.biblegateway.com/; http://www.biblestudytools.com/.

3. Determine the usage of the Hebrew word.

The number of times the word is used in the Bible, along with the places in the Bible where the word is found, have a great bearing on understanding meaning. For instance, if a word is only used one time in the Hebrew Bible, a comparative biblical study cannot be done. Sources from outside the Bible would have to be consulted to help determine its basic meaning. Still, the contextual clues from the Bible should confine the word's meaning somewhat. If a word is used an abundance of times, determining meaning is somewhat easier, since there are multiple opportunities for comparison. In this step, take note of how many times the word is used in your given chapter, in a given book of the Bible, and in a given section of the Bible such as the Pentateuch, the Prophets, or the Writings. Special note also should be taken if the word is used primarily in poetry, narrative, prophetic, or legal settings.

4. List all the English words used for that one Hebrew word.

Usually, there are only a few English words for any given Hebrew word. But that is not always the case. For example, the Hebrew word for "mercy" (חֶסֶד) is translated into more than ten English words in the King James Version. Such a high number of English words indicates the breadth and depth of the Hebrew word. Plus, it points out the difficulty of trying to capture that depth and breadth in English. This type of information is also found in Bible programs, lexicons, and concordances.

5. Consider how the contextual settings influenced each of the English word choices.

When possible, it is best to examine every contextual setting for each of the English word choices. But in the case of the Hebrew word (חֶסֶד), "mercy" is the most predominate translation choice. It was used over 140 times in the King James Version. In such a case, not all of the passages where "mercy" is used must be examined. But look at enough of them that you develop an understanding of why the contextual settings prompted the usage of the word "mercy."

5.5 Basic Vocabulary

אָרוֹן	= *ark, coffin, chest*
אֱמוּנָה	= *faithfulness, reliability*
הַר	= *hill, mountain, hill country*
חֶסֶד	= *mercy, loyalty, faithfulness, loving-kindness*
חָכָם	= *wise man*
יְלָדִים	= *children*
יְרוּשָׁלַיִם	= *Jerusalem*
רַע	= *evil, bad, wicked*

5.6 Exercises

1. Write out the summary of the definite article.

   _____

2. Write out the three inseparable prepositions.

   _____

3. Write out the summary of the Vav conjunction.

   _____

4. List the five steps of a word study process.

   _____

5. Using the nouns from the vocabulary of Chapters 4 and 5, write at least ten Hebrew nouns and attach the definite article. Use the summary in this chapter as a guideline.

6. Using the nouns from the vocabulary of Chapters 4 and 5, write at least ten Hebrew nouns and attach the three inseparable prepositions. Use the summary in this chapter as a guideline.

7. Using any of the words from the vocabulary of Chapters 4 and 5, write at least ten Hebrew words and attach the Vav conjunction. Use the summary in this chapter as a guideline.

Chapter 6

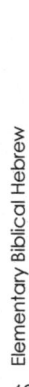

Pronouns, Construct States, and Adjectives

6.1 Pronouns

Simply put, pronouns are a small group of words that replace nouns. For instance, examine the sentences below.

Tom and Valorie built the house where he and she live. It is near my hometown and his parents. That house is very different from those in the neighboring city.

Let's examine the pronouns and their usage.

1. *Tom and Valorie built the house where he and she live.* This first sentence uses two pronouns: *he* and *she*. *He* and *she* refer back to Tom and Valorie, and are gender specific, independent words. The nouns being referred to are called antecedents.

2. *It is near my hometown and his parents.* This sentence uses three pronouns: *it, my,* and *his*. *It* refers back to the house and replaces the word *house*. *My* and *his* show possession of hometown and parents.

3. *That house is very different from those in the neighboring city.* Here, two pronouns are used: *that* and *those*. *That* and *those* are called demonstrative pronouns. Demonstrative pronouns show definiteness and particularity. The house is not just *a* house. It is *that* particular one. *Those* are the particular ones in the neighboring city.

Hebrew pronouns work in much the same way. Hebrew pronouns replace nouns, show possession, and tighten the definiteness and particularity of a noun.

6.1.1 Independent Personal Pronouns

We will now examine the Hebrew independent personal pronouns. First, independent personal pronouns are gender specific. There are masculine and feminine independent personal pronouns. There is also a common designation where the pronoun is the same for both genders. Second, independent personal pronouns have number; they are either singular or plural. Third, independent personal pronouns are based on person. *First* person is the person speaking or writing the sentence (I and we). *Second* person refers to the one or ones being addressed (you). *Third* person (he, she, it) refers to those not being addressed specifically (you) nor those speaking (I, we). For example, consider this sentence: *I am talking to you; he is not being addressed.* The first person is talking (I). The second person (you) is being addressed. The third person (he) is neither the one speaking nor the one being addressed.

There is a chart that develops from this concept that is used repeatedly in Hebrew grammar texts. Take the time to understand this chart completely.

Person and Gender	Singular Translation	Plural Translation	Abbreviation
1 Common (1c)	I	We	1cs and 1cp
2 Masculine (2m)	You	You	2ms and 2mp
2 Feminine (2f)	You	You	2fs and 2fp
3 Masculine (3m)	He/It	They	3ms and 3mp
3 Feminine (3f)	She/It	They	3fs and 3fs

Using this chart, the Hebrew independent personal pronouns are categorized below. Memorize the Hebrew words; their definition; and their person, gender, and number; in that specific order—person, gender, and number.

Person and Gender	Singular Translation	Plural Translation	Abbreviation
1 Common	I = אָנֹכִי, אֲנִי	We = אֲנַחְנוּ	1cs and 1cp
2 Masculine	You = אַתָּה	You = אַתֶּם	2ms and 2mp
2 Feminine	You = אַתְּ	You = אַתֵּנָה	2fs and 2fp
3 Masculine	He/It = הוּא	They = הֵמָּה, הֵם	3ms and 3mp
3 Feminine	She/It = הִיא, *הוּא	They = הֵנָּה, הֵן	3fs and 3fs

*This form is used only in the Pentateuch.

The Hebrew independent personal pronouns are used as the subjects in a sentence. They are the nouns that perform the action of the sentence.

The independent personal pronouns are also used in verbless clauses. In verbless clauses, there are no verbs. The "to be" verbs should be inserted.

Examples:

אָנֹכִי אֱלֹהִים	I am God (אָנֹכִי = 1cs)
אֲחֹתִי אַתְּ	You are my sister (אַתְּ = 2fs)
בָּנַי הֵם	They are my sons (הֵם = 3mp)

You will notice there is no verb in the examples. It is necessary to supply the "to be" verb (am, are) in each example. Also, you should note that the pronouns are in different places within the sentences. Both positions are common and acceptable.

6.1.2 Demonstrative Pronouns

Demonstrative pronouns show definiteness and particularity. The house is not just a house. It is *that* particular one. So the definiteness of an object is refined even more through the use of demonstrative pronouns. Demonstrative pronouns are also independent pronouns. They are standalone words. They do not have person, but do have gender and number. You will want to memorize the chart below.

Gender	Singular	Plural
Masculine	this = זֶה	these = אֵלֶה (common gender)
Feminine	this = זֹאת	these = אֵלֶה (common gender)
Masculine	that = הוּא	those = הֵם, הֵמָּה
Feminine	that = הִיא	those = הֵנָּה הֵן

Examples:

Psalms 24:10 =	"this king"	זֶה מֶלֶךְ	= ms
Deuteronomy 27:3 =	"this law"	הַתּוֹרָה הַזֹּאת	= fs (with definite article)
Genesis 34:21 =	"these men"	הָאֲנָשִׁים הָאֵלֶה	= cp (with definite article)

6.2 Pronominal Suffixes

Pronominal suffixes are suffixes added to nouns, prepositions, and verbs that represent a pronoun. When attached to nouns, pronominal suffixes indicate possession. For instance, pronominal suffixes added to the word "horse" would be translated as "my horse," "your horse," "our horse," and so on. Below are the suffixes added to the word סוּס = *horse*. These suffixes and forms should be memorized.

		Singular Nouns: Type 1 Suffixes				
1cs	סוּסִי	my horse		1cp	סוּסֵנוּ	our horse
2ms	סוּסְךָ	your horse		2mp	סוּסְכֶם	your horse
2fs	סוּסֵךְ	your horse		2fp	סוּסְכֶן	your horse
3ms	סוּסוֹ	his horse		3mp	סוּסָם	their horse
3fs	סוּסָהּ	her horse		3fp	סוּסָן	their horse

There is a different set of pronominal suffixes that are attached to plural nouns. These suffixes should be learned as well.

		Plural Nouns: Type 2 Suffixes				
1cs	סוּסַי	my horses		1cp	סוּסֵינוּ	our horses
2ms	סוּסֶיךָ	your horses		2mp	סוּסֵיכֶם	your horses
2fs	סוּסַיִךְ	your horses		2fp	סוּסֵיכֶן	your horses
3ms	סוּסָיו	his horses		3mp	סוּסֵיהֶם	their horses
3fs	סוּסֶיהָ	her horses		3fp	סוּסֵיהֶן	their horses

There are several similarities between the Type 1 suffixes—which are attached to singular nouns—and Type 2 suffixes—which are attached to plural nouns. When memorizing, it might be helpful to focus on those similarities. You also need to know that there are varying suffixes for some other nouns, prepositions, and verbs. Those suffixes are also similar in many cases and are recognizable once the suffixes above are memorized. For this stage of your learning, knowing the pronominal suffixes for masculine nouns will create a foundation for understanding the concept and practice of adding pronominal suffixes.

6.3 Construct States

Another way Hebrew shows possession is through noun construct states. In Hebrew sentence construction, the pronominal suffixes above are literally written "horse of mine," "horse of hers," and so on. The construct states show that same flow, but without the use of pronominal suffixes. In English we have the word "of" to demonstrate that close, possessive connection. In biblical Hebrew there is no word for "of." The method they used is called a construct state or a construct chain.

In construct chains, nouns are placed together in a chain of nouns, so to speak, sometimes with a Maqqef to show unity of function. Most often there are two nouns in a construct chain, but sometimes there are three. In the construct chain, the last noun in the chain is in an *absolute* state. The absolute state is the root form of the word found in lexicons. The other nouns in the construct chain, typically just one other noun, but sometimes two, are said to be in a *construct* state. The construct state is a shortened form (whenever possible) of the absolute form. Study the example below.

Example:

The construct chain above should be translated as "man of God." The construct state allows the reader to see the close and possessive connection between the words. Below are some biblical samples.

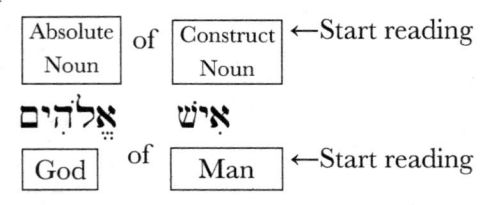

| Absolute Noun | of | Construct Noun | ←Start reading |

אֱלֹהִים אִישׁ

| God | of | Man | ←Start reading |

Examples:

מֶלֶךְ הָאָרֶץ = The king of the land (1 Sam. 21:11)

בֵּית־אֱלֹהִים = The house of God (Judges 18:31)

הַכֹּהֵן בֶּן־אַהֲרֹן = The priest of the son of Aaron (Neh. 10:38)

In the first two samples, you will note that the definiteness of the construct chain is determined by the absolute noun. The word מֶלֶךְ does not have the definite article. But the definite article is attached to הָאָרֶץ, which determines the definiteness of the chain. Thus, the translation is "the king of the land."

The last construct chain in the example above has three nouns. The first two nouns, priest and son, are considered to be in construct state. The last two are connected with the Maqqef. Despite the Maqqef, the last noun, Aaron, is in the absolute state. In this situation with three nouns in the chain, the word "of" is supplied between them all.

Construct nouns may sometimes have an inseparable preposition. In the example below, note the attached inseparable preposition on the construct noun. The preposition is translated normally.

Example:

לְבֵית אֱלֹהִים = for the house of God (Ezra 1:4)

6.4 Adjectives

Adjectives are words that tell something about a noun or pronoun. If you wanted to describe a noun, you might use words such as *good, bad, red, purple, righteous, evil, bright, dark,* and so forth. So, adjectives are modifying the noun that they accompany. Rather than just being a noun, the adjective reveals what kind of noun it is. Adjectives are used to paint word pictures so the reader can visualize that noun in descriptive and specific ways. Below are some examples of English adjectives used in the Bible.

Examples:

 1. Genesis 12:2   "I will make you a *great* nation."

 2. Genesis 1:24   "Let the earth bring forth *living* creatures."

 3. Isaiah 6:3   "*Holy, Holy, Holy,* is the Lord of hosts."

 4. Psalms 33:12   "*Blessed* is the nation whose God is the Lord."

 5. Deuteronomy 25:1 "They justify the *righteous* and condemn the *wicked.*"

 6. Psalms 115:17   "The *dead* do not praise the Lord."

Not only do these examples show us adjectives in a sentence, but I chose them because they also demonstrate three different uses of adjectives. The adjectives in examples 1 and 2 (*great* and *living*) are *attributive* adjectives. That is, they tell us an attribute of that noun. The nation is not just a nation, but a *great* nation. The creatures are not just any creatures, but *living* creatures. In the attributive use, adjectives will follow the noun and agree in number, gender, and definiteness.

Let's take a look at some simple examples in Hebrew.

Attributive adjectives follow the noun and agrees in number, gender, and definiteness.

סוּס טוֹב	= a good horse (טוֹב = *good*)
הַסּוּס הַטּוֹב	= the good horse (both have the definite article)
סוּסָה טוֹבָה	= a good mare (both have feminine suffixes)
הַסּוּסָה הַטּוֹבָה	= the good mare (both have suffixes and the definite article)

Examples 3 and 4 reveal a *predicative* use of adjectives. A predicate adjective in Hebrew is translated with the "to be" verb: "*Holy* is the Lord" and "*Blessed* is the nation." In the predicative use, the adjective will most often precede the noun. Furthermore, the predicate adjective will not take the definite article. So, predicate adjectives agree with their nouns in number and gender, but not necessarily in definiteness.

Predicative adjectives usually precede the noun and agree in number and gender but not definiteness.

טוֹב הַסּוּס	= the horse is good (literally "good is the horse")
קָדוֹשׁ הַיּוֹם	= the day is holy (קָדוֹשׁ = *holy*; "holy is the day")
חָכָם הַמֶּלֶךְ	= the king is wise (חָכָם = wise, skillful)

Examples 5 and 6 show the *substantive* use of adjectives. Substantive adjectives stand alone as a noun. In the samples, *the righteous, the wicked*, and *the dead* are adjectives that stand as nouns but are actually descriptive words. Often substantive adjectives are translated as "the righteous *ones*," "the wicked *ones*," or "the dead *ones*," in which case the noun *ones* is supplied and not a part of the actual Hebrew sentence.

Substantive adjectives are standalone nouns that have no accompanying noun to modify; the adjective becomes the noun.

קָדוֹשׁ	= holy one/man (masc.)
קְדוֹשִׁים	= holy ones
חָכָם	= wise one
חֲכָמָה	= wise woman (fem.)
חֲכָמִים	= wise men (masc.)

Summary of Adjectives:

1. **Attributive adjectives** follow the noun and agree in number, gender, and definiteness.

2. **Predicative adjectives** usually precede the noun and agree in number and gender, but not definiteness.

3. **Substantive adjectives** are standalone nouns that have no accompanying noun to modify; thus the adjective becomes the noun.

6.5 Basic Vocabulary

אַהֲרֹן	= Aaron
כֹּהֵן	= priest
טוֹב	= good
קָדוֹשׁ	= holy
אַחֵר	= another, other
גָּדוֹל	= great, big, large
חַי	= living, alive
צַדִּיק	= righteous, just
רַב	= great, many
רָשָׁע	= wicked, guilty
דָּוִד	= David
בָּבֶל	= Babylon
יַעֲקֹב	= Jacob
לֵוִי	= Levi
מִצְרַיִם	= Egypt
פְּלִשְׁתִּי	= Philistines
שָׁאוּל	= Saul
שְׁלֹמֹה	= Solomon
אַבְרָהָם	= Abraham
בַּעַל	= Baal

6.6 Exercises

1. Write out the independent pronouns.

2. Write out the demonstrative pronouns.

3. Write out the pronominal suffixes—both type 1 and type 2.

4. Using the steps in Chapter 5 and your favorite passage from the Bible, complete a word study for a noun.

5. Translate the following sentences. Use the biblical references on the right to check your translations.

a.	אֱלֹהִים אֲנִי	Genesis 35:11
b.	אֱלֹהֵיכֶם	Genesis 43:23
c.	יוֹם־יְהוָה הַגָּדוֹל	Zephaniah 1:14
d.	בַּיּוֹם הַהוּא (preposition בְּ)	Genesis 33:16
e.	הַר־קָדְשִׁי	Psalms 2:6
f.	הַדְּבָרִים הָאֵלֶּה	Genesis 15:1
g.	יְהוָה הַצַּדִּיק וַאֲנִי וְעַמִּי הָרְשָׁעִים	Exodus 9:27
h.	יְהוָה צַדִּיק	Psalms 129:4

Verbs: Part 1

7.1 Verbs

Verbs are the action or movement words of the sentence. Some have even said that verbs are the life, heart, and soul of a language. Verbs reveal what the subject is doing, what is being done to the subject, or the subject's state of being inside a sentence.

Examples:

1. The boat sailed. (Simple action—what the subject is doing.)

2. The boat was painted. (Passive action—what was done to the subject.)

3. The boat is old. (State of being—the subject's status.)

Besides action, verbs tell the reader a great deal of information. For instance, verbs have a component called *tense*. If the action is currently happening, it is in the present tense: *The boy is running. The boy runs.* If the action has already happened, it is in the past tense: *The boy ran. The boy has run. The boy was running.* If the action has not happened yet, it is in the future tense: *The boy will run.* While there are some other verb tenses, these three make up the vast majority.

Not only do verbs reveal a tense, they also make known types of action. In English we use adverbs to show the type of action. In Hebrew, however, the action types are shown through what is known as verbal stems. There are three types of action indicated in the Hebrew verbal stems: simple action, intense action, and causative action.

Examples:

1. The student wrote.

2. The students wrote intensely.

3. The teacher caused the students to write.

In the first example, no indication concerning the type of action is given. It is considered simple action. In the second, the adverb *intensely* is added to demonstrate the increased or heightened force of the action. The Hebrew stems themselves indicate that elevated intensity, instead of using an adverb. The last example shows causality. The teacher caused the action to happen, even though the action was completed by the students.

Hebrew verbal stems also indicate the voice of the action. There are three voices:

1. Active voice—the subject is acting

2. Passive voice—the subject is being acted upon

3. Reflexive voice—the subject is acting upon himself/herself

7.2 Hebrew Verbs: Part 1

7.2.1 Verb Stems

There are seven main Hebrew stems to express various types of actions. Those seven are called Qal, Niphal, Piel, Pual, Hithpael, Hiphil, and Hophal. You will encounter other stems in reference material, but these seven are the most common stems you will encounter. The verbal stems can be set up in a matrix. You should memorize it.

		Action		
		Simple	**Intensive**	**Causative**
Voice	**Active**	*Qal*	*Piel*	*Hiphil*
	Passive	*Niphal*	*Pual*	*Hophal*
	Reflexive	*Niphal*	*Hithpael*	

From this verbal matrix, we can make the following statements:

1. *Qal* is a Simple Active stem. The subject simply acts according to the nature of the verb.

2. *Piel* is an Intensive Active stem. The subject acts with greater intensity.[14] Recently, scholars have pointed out that a single, identifying usage for the Piel stem has been elusive, although most recognize that the Piel stem is used in a variety of ways besides showing intensity. But for now, identify the Piel as intensive.

3. *Hiphil* is a Causative Active stem. The subject causes the action, although the action may be completed by another.

4. *Niphal* is most often a Simple Passive stem. The subject is being acted upon simply.

5. *Pual* is an Intensive Passive stem. The subject is being acted upon with an elevated intensity.

6. *Hophal* is a Causative Passive stem. The subject is being caused to do something. The causative force is not the subject.

7. *Niphal* can also be a Simple Reflexive action, where the subject acts upon itself. The context of the verb and sentence will be the determining factors as to whether the Niphal is passive or reflexive.

8. *Hithpael* is the Intensive Reflexive. The subject is acting upon itself with an elevated intensity.

Like English verbs, Hebrew verbs are inflected. Inflection is the adding of letters to verbs to nuance the action. For instance, we can inflect the verb *walk* by adding *s*, *ed*, and *ing*: *walks*, *walked*, and *walking*. Each of these inflections represents a different nuance of the verb. In similar manner, every Hebrew stem is inflected according to the stem characteristics. Those inflections (stems) become the identifying characteristic of the verb and will determine its proper translation.

Verbal inflections are added to the root or lexical forms. Most Hebrew verbal roots are tri-literal, which means the root is made up of three consonants. Roots where the three consonants remain unchanged during inflection are called strong verbs. Weak verbs are made up of roots where the consonants may change during stem inflections.[15] A verb is considered weak if it has one of three characteristics:

---

14 Other uses for the Piel include factitive (causing a state), denominative (a verb derived from a noun), frequentative (iterative, pluralistic, and intensive), or declarative (proclamation). See Bill T. Arnold and John H. Choi, *A Guide to Biblical Hebrew Syntax* (Cambridge: Cambridge University Press, 2003).

15 Although a majority of Hebrew verbs are weak, the enormous scope of the weak verb formations dictate that our focus in this text remains primarily on the strong verb.

1. A root consonant is a guttural א, ה, ח, ע, or ר.

2. The verb begins with י, ו, or נ.

3. The second and third consonant are the same.

7.2.2 Stem Inflections

The verbal inflections for each stem are different. So, by learning the characteristic inflection of each stem, we can translate the verbs correctly. Historically, Hebrew teachers chose to use the tri-literal, strong root קָטַל as a model for the various inflections. The word means "to kill." Below are the 3ms inflections for each stem added to the stem chart from 7.2.1.

		Action		
		Simple	**Intensive**	**Causative**
Voice	**Active**	*Qal* קָטַל	*Piel* קִטֵּל	*Hiphil* הִקְטִיל
	Passive	*Niphal* נִקְטַל	*Pual* קֻטַּל	*Hophal* הָקְטַל
	Reflexive	*Niphal* נִקְטַל	*Hithpael* הִתְקַטֵּל	

7.2.3 Stem Diagnostics

1. **Qal.** In the Qal, the root is inflected with the Qamets and the Pathach. Pay attention to the correlations between the vowels used in the Hebrew inflection and the stem name. The name Qal is spelled with an "a class" vowel. In the Hebrew, the Qal stem in the 3ms uses "a class" vowels—the Pathach and Qamets. The stem name reveals the vowels used in the inflection of the 3ms. The same pattern holds true for all 3ms inflections of strong, tri-literal roots.

2. **Piel.** In the Piel, the root is inflected with the Hireq and the Tsere, again as indicated in the name Piel. Another feature of the Piel is the addition of the Dagesh Forte in the second consonant of the root.

3. **Hiphil.** The Hiphil is inflected with the vowel Hireq Yod and the addition of the He as a prefix. Once again, the name Hiphil reveals the vowels and inclusion of the He. You should also be aware that the Sheva under the first root consonant is a syllable marker and is silent.

4. **Niphal.** The Niphal is inflected, as its name reveals, with the vowels Hireq and Pathach. It also includes a Nun prefix. The Sheva under the first root consonant is a syllable marker and is silent.

> **Note:** The Niphal is also used as Simple Reflexive and is inflected the same. Only the context will determine whether the verb should be translated as Simple Passive or Simple Reflexive.

5. **Pual.** The Pual is inflected using the vowels Shureq and Pathach. As with the Piel, the Pual includes a Dagesh Forte in the second consonant of the root.

6. **Hophal.** The Hophal is inflected using the vowels Qamets Hatuf and the Pathach. As the name suggests, there is also a prefixed He. The Sheva under the first root consonant is a syllable marker and is silent.

7. **Hithpael.** The Hithpael is inflected using the vowels Pathach and Tsere. As with the other intensive verbs, the Hithpael has a Dagesh Forte in the second consonant of the root. Hithpael also includes the הִתְ as a prefix. The Sheva under the Tav is a syllable marker and is silent.

		Action		
		Simple	**Intensive**	**Causative**
Voice	**Active**	*Qal* קָטַל	*Piel* קִטֵּל	*Hiphil* הִקְטִיל
	Passive	*Niphal* נִקְטַל	*Pual* קֻטַּל	*Hophal* הָקְטַל
	Reflexive	*Niphal* נִקְטַל	*Hithpael* הִתְקַטֵּל	

7.3 Word Studies: Hebrew Verbs

When carrying out a word study on a Hebrew verb, first complete steps 1 and 2 found in Chapter 5 (section 5.4) for nouns. Once those steps are completed, continue to the steps below.

1. **Determine the Hebrew verb stem.**

   A word study on a Hebrew verb should seek to understand the various nuances of that verb. The verb stems are crucial to that understanding. The same verb is often found with a variety of stems. By using various stems, the author is attempting to capture different nuances of action.

   Consider these sentences: *Jeremy played basketball. Caleb played music. Kasey played with her daughter.* In all these examples, the verb is "played." But you will note that even though the word is the same in each sentence, the meaning of the action is a bit different. Playing basketball is different than playing music. Playing with one's daughter has a different nuance than playing basketball or playing music, although that nuanced meaning could include playing both music and basketball. Hebrew verbs are used in a similarly nuanced manner. Determining the verb stem is the first step to the proper understanding of your word.

   As stated in Chapter 5, free, online resources, lexicons, and word studies are available to use in this step. Many digital sources will let you hover a computer cursor over words, which will then produce a drop-down box with all the pertinent information. Again, I personally recommend free online Bibles for this step. It is the simplest and cheapest way to get to the Hebrew from the English text.

2. **List all the English words used for that Hebrew verbal root.**

   While this seems like a reversal of process, it is not. By listing all the English words the translators used for that one Hebrew word for that one particular root, you will begin to see its full range of meaning. Some verbs will have a more focused range of meaning. Others will be far ranging in meaning. Listing all the English words used for that one Hebrew word helps you mentally establish its range of meaning.

3. **Note any changes in meaning if the verb changes stem.**

   There are some cases where the meaning of a verb will change in different stems. For instance, the word יָרָה means *to throw, cast, shoot arrows* in the Qal stem. In the Niphal, it means *to be shot*. In the Hiphil it can also mean those things, but the range extends further. The general range of meaning is throwing or casting something like arrows, water, stones, and so on. The word's more direct and focused meaning in certain contexts is *to point out, show, direct, teach,* or *instruct*. Thus, we begin to understand that the word יָרָה has a range that includes a person casting knowledge to a learner. And since the change is in the Hiphil, a causal stem, the range could extend to mean that a person casts knowledge in a way that causes another to learn.

   If we didn't list and analyze the English meanings and note any changes in meaning if the verb changes stem, we would sorely misunderstand the action יָרָה. One such time is when God was speaking to Moses and said, "I will be with your mouth, and teach you what you are to say" (Ex 4:12; NASB). If we applied the meaning of יָרָה in the Qal stem to the context of Exodus 4:12, the meaning of the sentence would be nonsense! God would say to Moses, "I will be with your mouth and throw, cast, or shoot arrows for what you are to say." It makes no sense at all. Therefore, when conducting a word study for a verb, list the English words used by the translators and note any changes of meaning when the stems change.

4. Consider how the contextual settings influenced each of the English word choices.

Consider once again these sentences: *Jeremy played basketball. Caleb played music. Kasey played with her daughter.* The context around the verb "played" influences the verb's exact, nuanced meaning. In Hebrew it is no different.

Using the word יָרָה, God told Moses He would teach (Hiphil stem) him what to say. In Psalms 64:3–4, David says that his enemies have "aimed bitter speech as their arrow, to shoot from concealment at the blameless" (NASB). In the context of David's psalm, the same Hebrew word יָרָה is used, but in the Qal stem. The context has determined the exact nuanced meaning of the word. Always seek to understand how context has influenced the meaning of the Hebrew words.

7.4 Word Study Summary

Word Study Process

Nouns	Verbs
1. Select only the most important words for your study.	1. Complete Steps 1 and 2 for nouns.
2. Determine the Hebrew word from which the English word was derived.	2. Determine the Hebrew verb stem.
3. Determine the usage of the Hebrew word.	3. List all the English words used for that Hebrew verb root.
4. List all the English words used for that one Hebrew word.	4. Note any changes in meaning if the verb changes stem.
5. Consider how the contextual settings influenced each of the English word choices.	5. Consider how the contextual settings influenced each of the English word choices.

The best practice when doing word studies, whether it be nouns or verbs, would be to validate our findings with other scholars. So, make it a habit to look at what other scholars say about the word in the particular text you are studying. Check with word studies (lexicons, concordances, dictionaries) to see if they point out your text in their definitions. Read commentaries, both technical and devotional, to see what those scholars might say about your word. Doing this will protect you from going astray.

7.5 Basic Hebrew Vocabulary

דָּבַר = *to speak or say*

מָלַךְ = *to rule or reign*

פָּקַד = *to attend to, pay attention to, take care of*

כָּרַת = *to cut a covenant, cut off, cut down*

כָּתַב = *to write, register, record*

שָׁכַב = *to lie down, have sexual relations*

קָדַשׁ = *to be holy, consecrated, set apart*

שָׁמַר = *to keep, guard, watch over*

שָׁפַט = *to judge, decide, make a judgment*

דָּרַשׁ = *to seek, ask, inquire*

Note: All of the words are listed as the Qal 3ms forms. Thus they can be translated as "he reigned"; "he judged"; "he was holy"; et cetera.

7.6 Exercises

Translate the following sentences into English. Follow the rules and vocabulary of the previous chapters.

1. מָלַךְ הַמֶּלֶךְ הַטּוֹב

2. וְכָתַב דָּוִד כָּל אֵלֶּה דְּבָרִים

3. שָׁמַר הָרוּחַ הָאָרוֹן אֱלֹהִים

_____

4. שָׁפַת הוּא עַל הַר

_____

5. פָּקַד יַעֲקֹב סוּסֵיהֶם

_____

6. בְּבָל כָּרַת בְּמִצְרַיִם

_____

7.7 Further Reading

Arnold, Bill T., and John H. Choi. 2003. *A Guide to Biblical Hebrew Syntax.* Cambridge: Cambridge University Press.

Chapter 8

Verbs: Part 2

8.1 Verb Tenses and the Qal Perfect Conjugation

8.1.1 Verb Tenses

Verb tenses are often understood to be the time of the action. For instance, in English, the present tense represents action that is happening in the present: *Boys run. The boy is running.* The past tense is action in the past: *The boy ran.*

In the examples above, the verbal root is *run*. Notice that the word *run* was changed to *running* and *ran* to demonstrate different tenses. That change is called *conjugating* or inflecting a word. A conjugated verb is one that has been modified to indicate a new grammatical usage. Conjugations occur for person, number, gender, voice, and type of action, as well as the tense. Nouns can be conjugated for number and gender, too.

In Hebrew strong verbs, inflections/conjugations of the verbal root occur through vowel changes or through adding suffixes and prefixes. In Hebrew weak verbs, however, not only will prefixes and suffixes be added, there will also be some consonant changes. All of these changes reflect a change in the root word's grammatical use in the sentence.

In Hebrew, the entire grouping of verbal root modifications, which are by and large repeatable in other strong verbs, is called a conjugation. For instance, there are eight verb stems, as discussed in Chapter 7. Each of these stems has a pattern of inflection. There is a pattern of inflection for the Qal, Piel, Pual, and so on.

Furthermore, there are eight verb tenses: perfect, imperfect, imperative, cohortative, jussive, infinitive construct, infinitive absolute, and the participle, which will be studied below. All of these tenses are inflected in certain repeatable patterns for each of the verb stems. Thus, there is a Qal perfect conjugation, a Qal imperfect conjugation, a Piel participle conjugation, and so on. All of those variables create a large number of conjugations for Hebrew verbs. Thus, the Hebrew language student must spend a great deal of time and effort learning and recognizing those verbal conjugations.

For our purposes in this text, we will simply learn the most basic forms of קָטַל for each verb tense, and not the entire conjugation. By doing so, we will be learning the grammatical intent of each verb tense, as well as the most basic inflection that occurs in that particular conjugation. We will, however, need to learn and memorize the entire Qal perfect conjugation for קָטַל.

The Perfect

While Hebrew verb tenses do include a time element, the most important function of the Hebrew perfect verb tense is to reflect the completion of an action. Consider the English sentence, *Cain slew Abel*. The verbal root means "to slay." By using the modified form slew, we have inflected the verb and changed its grammatical function to indicate an action that is now complete. Since the action is complete, the translation will be as a simple action that has occurred already (i.e., as action in the past, although the emphasis is on the completed aspect of the action).

In Genesis 1:1, we are told, "God created the heavens and the earth." The root word for "created" is בָּרָא, meaning "to create." In the English translation, you will note that we inflected "create" into "created," showing completed action in the past. In Hebrew verbs, inflections do the same. The inflection of the word בָּרָא is part of the Qal perfect conjugation and is inflected according to that pattern of inflection. The entire Qal perfect conjugation will be demonstrated below.

The Imperfect

The imperfect tense indicates an incomplete action. Often the incomplete action is translated with a future time component. But the emphasis is the incomplete action. To demonstrate the incompleteness, the verbs are often accompanied by helping words such as *will, should, could, might,* and so on.

Consider the sentence: *Teresa will manage a large corporation*. In the sentence, the action is not yet completed and thus is translated as a future action. Yet, in Hebrew, the emphasis is not on the time element but on the incompleteness of the action.

Here is a biblical example. Genesis 2:18 says, "I will make him a helper suitable for him" (NASB). The verb "will make" is from the root word עָשָׂה, meaning "to do, or make." It is inflected to be a Qal imperfect form in this sentence. Thus, the translator used the word "will make" to show that the action had not yet been completed at that point in the story, even though the entire story is in our (the reader's) past. Thus, the emphasis is on incomplete action.

The imperfect is often described as the prefix conjugation, whereas the perfect is a suffix conjugation. This is because the primary identifier of the imperfect is the addition of the prefixes י, ה, א, or נ. You can see this clearly in the Qal imperfect 3ms form.

Example:

| Qal perfect 3ms | = | קָטַל | *he killed* |
| Qal imperfect 3ms | = | יִקְטֹל | *he will kill* |

Imperative

Imperatives are commands, desires, and wishes. The Hebrew imperative conjugation expresses second-person commands. Ponder these: *Go away. Stay here. Play harder. Swing higher.* These are all imperatives. The subject of the sentence is issuing commands that express his or her desires. In effect, the subject is saying, *You go away. You stay here. You play harder. You swing higher.* The imperative then is considered a second-person command and inflected in the second person.

Being a second-person command, the imperative is inflected like the imperfect second-person forms, minus the prefix. Here are the imperative forms.

Example:

Qal perfect 3ms	=	קָטַל	*he killed*
Qal imperfect 3ms	=	יִקְטֹל	*he will kill*
Qal imperative 2ms	=	קְטֹל	*you (masculine) kill*
2fs	=	קִטְלִי	*you (feminine) kill*

Cohortative

Much like the imperative, the cohortative expresses a will or desire of the subject, but includes himself or herself. The sentence, *Let's do this*, is a type of cohortative. It expresses the desire and will of the subject but includes himself or herself in the command. The cohortative is inflected as a first-person verb and includes the subject and others.

The cohortative is inflected like the first-person imperfect. The position of the verb in its setting will indicate whether the verb is cohortative or first-person imperfect.

Example:

Qal perfect 3ms	=	קָטַל	*he killed*
Qal imperfect 3ms	=	יִקְטֹל	*he will kill*
Qal imperative 2ms	=	קְטֹל	*you (masculine) kill*
2fs	=	קִטְלִי	*you (feminine) kill*
Qal cohortative 1cs	=	אֶקְטְלָה	*let me kill*

Jussive

Like the imperative and cohortative, the jussive expresses a command, desire, or will. As the imperative is the second-person command, and the cohortative is the first-person command, the jussive is a third-person expression of desire or command.

Genesis 16:5 is an example of this type of third-person command. Sarah says to Abram, "May the Lord judge between you and me" (NASB). Sarah is saying, "I desire that the Lord (he = third person) judge between you and me." It is Sarah's desire that the Lord judge the situation.

Like the cohortative, the jussive is inflected like the third-person imperfect forms. As was the case with the cohortative, the jussive is identified from the imperfect by its position in the clause.

Example:

Qal perfect 3ms	=	קָטַל	*he killed*
Qal imperfect 3ms	=	יִקְטֹל	*he will kill*
Qal imperative 2ms	=	קְטֹל	*you (masculine) kill*
2fs	=	קִטְלִי	*you (feminine) kill*
Qal cohortative 1cs	=	אֶקְטְלָה	*let me kill*
Qal jussive 3ms	=	יִקְטֹל	*let him kill*

To summarize, the jussive is the third-person expression of desire and command, the imperative is the second-person expression of command and desire, while the cohortative is the first-person expression of command and desire.

Infinitive Construct

Infinitives are the base forms of a verb. For example, *to go, to eat, to create, to write*, are infinitives. These forms do not limit themselves to person, number, or gender. They are infinitive. Infinitives can be used in different ways in a sentence. One of the more famous infinitive statements ever made came from the lips of Hamlet: "To be or not to be, that is the question." In this sentence, the infinitive *to be* works as the object of the sentence. Let's rearrange it to see clearer. "The question is *to be* or not *to be*." The infinitive *to be* is actually a verb. But in the sentence it is acting in the place of a noun.

Another example would be the sentence, "You want to learn." As we break down the sentence, you is the subject, *want* is the verb, and *to learn* is the object, which in this case is an infinitive.

In Hebrew, the infinitive construct is a verbal noun. It is a verb form used in a sentence like a noun. It is often translated with the preposition "to" as in English. The infinitive construct is identical to the Qal imperative 2ms. The only way to differentiate between them is the context of the sentence.

Example:

Qal perfect 3ms	=	קָטַל *he killed*
Qal imperfect 3ms	=	יִקְטֹל *he will kill*
Qal imperative 2ms	=	קְטֹל *you (masculine) kill*
2fs	=	קִטְלִי *you (feminine) kill*
Qal cohortative 1cs	=	אֶקְטֹל *let me kill*
Qal jussive 3ms	=	יִקְטֹל *let him kill*
Qal infinitive	=	קְטֹל *to kill*

Infinitive Absolute

The infinitive absolute doesn't have an English equivalent, but IT also acts as a verbal noun. Unlike the infinitive construct, the infinitive absolute will not take prefixes, suffixes, or pronominal suffixes, and does not have the same function as the infinitive construct.

In Hebrew, the infinitive absolute has a few different functions and is quite often used in conjunction with other verbs. It can emphasize the intensity of an action—like an adverb. Infinitive absolutes may highlight a command when used with another verb. Also, infinitive absolutes are used to show action happening contemporaneously.

The infinitive absolute is identified from the infinitive construct by the Qamets in the first syllable. The translation of the infinitive absolute will be structured by its function in the sentence.

Example:

Qal perfect 3ms	=	קָטַל *he killed*
Qal imperfect 3ms	=	יִקְטֹל *he will kill*
Qal imperative 2ms	=	קְטֹל *you (masculine) kill*
2fs	=	קִטְלִי *you (feminine) kill*
Qal cohortative 1cs	=	אֶקְטֹל *let me kill*
Qal jussive 3ms	=	יִקְטֹל *let him kill*
Qal infinitive	=	קְטֹל *to kill*
Qal infinitive absolute	=	קְטֹל or קָטוֹל *to kill*

Participle

Participles are verbs that are used as adjectives or nouns. For example, look at these sentences: *Running horses are beautiful. Shooting stars flash across the sky.* In the sentence structure, *horses* and *stars* are the subjects. The words *running* and *shooting* are adjectives but their roots are from the verbal roots "to run" and "to shoot." Thus, participles are a verbal adjective.

Participles may also act as nouns. Consider the sentence, *I dislike dieting*. The participle is *dieting* and is a derivative of the verb "to diet." But in this sentence, it acts as a noun or the object being disliked. Participles may also be used as the subject of the sentence. For example, *Painting expresses one's soul.* The subject *painting* is used in the place of a noun, but is a derivative of the verbal root "to paint."

In Hebrew, participles function in a similar fashion. And like other Hebrew adjectives, participles may be used in attributive, predicative, and substantive situations. (See Chapter 6.) The participle does not have person, but does have gender and number. Furthermore, the participle has an active and passive voice. The forms below are the Qal active participle ms form and the Qal passive participle ms form. The translation of the participles will be structured by their exact function in the sentence.

Example:

Qal perfect 3ms	=	קָטַל *he killed*
Qal imperfect 3ms	=	יִקְטֹל *he will kill*
Qal imperative 2ms	=	קְטֹל *you (masculine) kill*
2fss	=	קִטְלִי *you (feminine) kill*
Qal cohortative 1cs	=	אֶקְטֹל *let me kill*
Qal jussive 3ms	=	יִקְטֹל *let him kill*
Qal infinitive	=	קְטֹל *to kill*
Qal infinitive absolute	=	קָטֹל or קָטוֹל *to kill*
Qal active participle ms	=	קֹטֵל *killing*
Qal passive participle ms	=	קָטוּל *killed*

8.1.2 The Qal Perfect Conjugation for Strong Roots

The Qal is a Simple Active stem. The subject simply acts according to the nature of the verb. The perfect tense communicates completed action and is usually translated as past tense. Remember, a conjugation is an entire set of inflections, which exist for every stem within each tense. The conjugation demonstrates how the inflections should be translated regarding person, number, and gender. Thus, the Qal perfect conjugation is the entire set of inflected forms of a verbal root that indicate person, gender, and number of a simple, completed action.

Verbal roots are inflected according to stem characteristics, tense, and whether or not the root is strong or weak. The magnitude of studying all the subsequent possibilities is quite enormous. So, for this elementary level, only the Qal strong conjugation will be demonstrated and should be memorized.

The Qal perfect conjugation is often called the *suffix conjugation* because the Qal perfect is inflected by adding suffixes to the verbal roots. The suffixes along with the ensuing vowel inflections reveal the translation of the Qal perfect verb.

Below is the Qal perfect conjugation for the word קָטַל = *to kill*. This strong verbal root was chosen long ago as a model for verbal paradigms and remains so in textbooks today. So, let's begin by looking at the Qal perfect conjugation of קָטַל. Memorizing the chart below is a necessary method for learning the other conjugations. Thus, you will want to memorize the Qal perfect conjugation for קָטַל. Pay particular attention to the suffixes added to emphasize person, number, and gender.

Remember that the Qal stem is uses the Qamets and Pathach as its vowels. The Qal paradigm below should be translated as simple past.

	Qal Perfect Conjugation	
	Strong Root	Translation
3ms	קָטַל	He killed
3fs	קָטְלָה	She killed
2ms	קָטַלְתָּ	You killed
2fs	קָטַלְתְּ	You killed
1cs	קָטַלְתִּי	I killed
3cp	קָטְלוּ	They killed
2mp	קְטַלְתֶּם	You killed
2fp	קְטַלְתֶּן	You killed
1cp	קָטַלְנוּ	We killed

The suffixes and patterns of vowel change are transferrable to all strong verbal roots. Notice the similar patterns of inflection in the Qal perfect conjugation for the words מָלַךְ and כָּתַב. Memorizing the patterns will be helpful for the study of other conjugations. As you compare the conjugations below, first read the 3ms of one verb, then read the 3ms of the other. Proceed throughout the chart in a similar fashion. Doing so will highlight the pattern of inflection.

Qal Perfect Conjugation		
Strong Root		Translation
3ms	מָלַךְ	He reigned
3fs	מָלְכָה	She reigned
2ms	מָלַכְתָּ	You reigned
2fs	מָלַכְתְּ	You reigned
1cs	מָלַכְתִּי	I reigned
3cp	מָלְכוּ	They reigned
2mp	מְלַכְתֶּם	You reigned
2fp	מְלַכְתֶּן	You reigned
1cp	מָלַכְנוּ	We reigned

Qal Perfect Conjugation		
Strong Root		Translation
3ms	כָּתַב	He wrote
3fs	כָּתְבָה	She wrote
2ms	כָּתַבְתָּ	You wrote
2fs	כָּתַבְתְּ	You wrote
1cs	כָּתַבְתִּי	I wrote

Qal Perfect Conjugation		
3cp	כָּתְבוּ	They wrote
2mp	כְּתַבְתֶּם	You wrote
2fp	כְּתַבְתֶּן	You wrote
1cp	כָּתַבְנוּ	We wrote

8.2 Basic Hebrew Vocabulary

רוּם = *to be high, exalted, arise, rise*

סָבַב = *to turn around, turn, go around*

שָׁבַר = *to break, break up, shatter*

רָדַף = *to pursue, follow after, chase*

קָבַר = *to bury*

8.3 Exercises

1. Write out the Qal perfect conjugation of קָטַל from memory. Work on it until you can do the entire conjugation.

2. Using the guideline in Chapter 5, complete a word study for a noun of your choice. The nouns from your favorite Old Testament passage would be a good place to begin.

3. Using the guidelines in Chapter 7, complete a word study for a verb of your choice. The verbs from your favorite Old Testament passage would be a good place to begin.

---

4. Translate the following words and phrases. All of the verbs are Qal stem verbs:

---

a. מָלַכְתִּי

b. כָּתַבְתְּ

c. קָטַלְתֶּם

d. יִקְטֹל (two options)

e. קָטַל

f. קָבַר אַהֲרֹן אֲרוֹן

g. קָטַל דָּוִד רַב פְּלִשְׁתִּי

h. מָלַךְ שָׁאוּל בִּירוּשָׁלַיִם

i. רוּם הַכֹּהֵן יהוה

j. רָדַף שָׁאוּל דָּוִד

k. שָׁבַר אֱלֹהִים בְּכָל רָע

CPSIA information can be obtained
at www.ICGtesting.com
Printed in the USA
LVOW03s0952120117
520716LV00012B/197/P

9 781631 892110